MW00416890

"My company has invested over $40 million into real estate deals with Jim's Team and has had great success. I also consider him one of my top advisors when it comes to living a legendary family life. He's a crowd favorite at our annual event."

Don Wenner, DLP Capital

"Southern Impression Homes helps White Coat Investors find new construction turnkey homes that they want to invest in. There's a whole lot of different ways to invest in real estate, and everybody's kind of got to find their place on the spectrum. Some people like to keep it very, very passive. The nice thing about a new construction turnkey home is that it's kind of in the middle of the spectrum. It allows people to get all the benefits of completely owning the home, while keeping the ownership as passive as possible. Let's be honest doctors are busy so a new construction turnkey option is a great solution for many of them."

Jim Dahle, White Coat Investor

"I have known and worked with Jim Sheils for the last eight years. He is a talented, hard working, successful real estate investor. When I first met him, he was working to make ends meet. Through perseverance, a great partnership, and shrewd investments he is successful and still growing. His business brings integrity and commitment to doing the right thing for the people who invest with him. I would be happy to communicate further if needed."

Keith Cunningham, KJC Investments

"If you pull the trigger now, you can start getting the tax benefits now and counting appreciation. That's what we finally did and now we're going to set ourselves up to be completely independent going forward."

David & Gina Nelson

"Don't hesitate, jump in. You just need to start."

Amina Goodwin

"Jim and Jamie's *Passive Income Playbook* has changed our life for the better. The real estate investments we've made through their build-to-rent program has accelerated our passive income to help give us the space to enjoy our family lives to the fullest. We've participated in their family masterminds. My wife, Camron, is part of their realtor referral program. Jamie even helped coach her through her last pregnancy. They've opened up their immense rolodex of personal and business contacts to us. Absolute game changers and some of my favorite people to work with."

Adam Hamilton

"I just want boring stuff that doesn't take up my time. New construction has been really good and didn't create a second job for me. And that's as important as the financial returns. It's a really exciting, boring investment!"

Tom Tousignant

"Jim – I am overwhelmed and grateful for you investing the rhythms into my family. To call it game-changing is an understatement. Your teaching and encouragement has impacted my family's life forever. Thank you."

John Ruhlin

"Jim and Jamie have the best actions and principles I have ever seen for entrepreneurs with family. By building Rhythms into our week, we now have more time, more connected conversations, and a relationship that is beyond what I ever thought possible. My family life is richer than I could have ever dreamed."

Rick Sapio

"This might sound harsh – but I believe our traditional educational system is letting us down. Even though my family lives in one of the top school districts in the country but I truly cannot say with confidence my kids are learning the most important skills for the 21st century. Learning from Jim and Jamie, we've started applying key concepts and ideas in our family to develop deeper bonds, connections, and shared values. I highly recommend their work."

Yanik Silver, Founder of Maverick1000 and Author of Evolved Enterprise

"Jim & Jamie Sheils have been regular contributors at our Fambundance Family Mastermind events and, each time, they bring deep wisdom and value to our families. They not only gave us the wake up call we needed about how important it is to cherish the limited time we have with our family, but they provide practical methods and tools that can be immediately implemented for meaningful results."

Mike McCarthy

"I initially met Jim and Jamie through the work they were doing with entrepreneur families. I was so impressed with their Build-To-Rent venture that I invested in, I ended up doubling my investment. I encouraged family members to invest in their Build-To-Rent program. Our returns have been excellent"

David Phelps, Freedom Founders

PASSIVE INCOME
PLAYBOOK

Leverage Built-to-Rent Real Estate to Buy Back
Your Time & Create a Legendary Family Life

PASSIVE INCOME
PLAYBOOK

Leverage Built-to-Rent Real Estate to Buy Back
Your Time & Create a Legendary Family Life

Jim & Jamie Sheils

ethos
collective

Published by Ethos Collective™
PO Box 43, Powell, OH 43065
www.ethoscollective.vip

LCCN: 2023909496
Paperback ISBN: 978-1-63680-172-8
Hardcover ISBN: 978-1-63680-173-5
e-Book ISBN: 978-1-63680-174-2

Available in paperback, hardcover, e-book, and audiobook.

Other Books by
Jim and Jamie Sheils

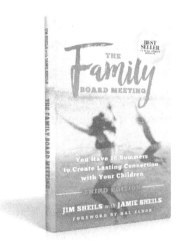

Dedication & Gratitude

Immense appreciation and celebration to our BTR partner, Chris Funk. You are the spreadsheet to our whiteboard.

Without our incredible team in Southern Impression Homes and 18 Summers, this journey would be impossible, thank you.

Our 5 spirited children, you are our inspiration. Thank you for making our life legendary.

Contents

Foreword   1

Introduction   7

Part 1: The Power of Passive   15

1. The First 2 Laws of Passive Income   17

2. The Third Law of Passive Income   27

3. The Power of New   39

Part 2: Build-To-Rent   51

4. The 5 Success Indicators   53

5. The 5 Traps   65

6. The BTR Storyline   77

7. Build to Live   91

Part 3: Build To Live   101

8. The Legendary Family Elements   103

9. The 4 Rhythms   117

10. The Passive Income Playbook   129

11. Legendary   139

Epilogue   145

Before you go   147

Appendix A: The BTR Investor Process   149

Appendix B: International Investors   155

Endnotes   159

About the Authors   161

Foreword

I bought my first home when I was 23.

I was working in real estate, and I'd learned enough to know that renting forever didn't make sense. As a young agent, I also believed that if I was going to sell houses, I should probably own one, too.

Still, it was the biggest purchase I'd ever made, and I was doing it alone. To make it work, I found a place with a basement apartment I could rent out. That relieved some of the pressure—the basement money took the sting out of the mortgage, and I slept a lot better as a result.

For a year, that was pretty much all it was: someone in the basement helping pay the bills.

By the following year, I was feeling more confident. When a similar property came on the market, I jumped on it. Suddenly, I had two homes and three tenants.

That's when everything changed. When I started cashing those new rent checks, I realized I wasn't just getting help with the bills from a guy in my basement anymore. That rent money was *income*. I had a *business*.

What's more, that money showed up every month. I was finding success as an agent in those early days, but commissions still went up and down. I'd have good months and not-so-good months. But that income showed up like clockwork. Better still, it showed up even if I didn't.

That was when I *really* understood passive income. And I've never looked back.

I've always bought for cash flow. I never believed I could tell if real estate values were going up or down in the short run. I don't think anyone can. But if there was income coming in each month, the value of the property didn't matter much. If my rental properties went down in value, I'd still get the same passive income. That gave me a sense of freedom in a way that work and other investments didn't. And that freedom *mattered*.

Passive income has always been a means for me, not an end. It's a tool. It's allowed me to live the life I want and, most importantly, to focus on the relationships that matter most.

In that way, Jim, Jamie, and I are kindred spirits. I've visited them at their home and toured their properties. I've driven ATVs through the construction roads of their newest developments and shared meals around their table. But what we share most is the belief that *people are what matter*. Relationships are the essence of what it means to thrive.

That belief is what led me to co-found Gobundance, the community for high-achieving entrepreneurs, executives, and thought leaders. It's kept me connected to my family and my peers. And it's allowed me to live an incredibly rich life filled with adventure and best of all, people.

I was fortunate to discover passive income early, and it's made the most important things in my life possible. My hope is that this book does the same for you.

Stay connected,
Pat Hiban, Co-Founder of Gobundance

Before we get started...

Hi!

Before you dive in, we've created an entire toolbox of resources to help you use our blueprint to generate passive income and build your legendary family life.

It's all free and all yours.

Just visit jjplaybook.com or scan the code below!

—*Jim & Jamie*

Introduction

A few years ago, we loaded our family into an RV the size of a small school bus and hit the open road.

For a family of seven, we've seen a lot of adventure. Thanks to the success of our approach to passive income, we've been able to travel the world, homeschool our kids, live in the tropics, and remain incredibly connected as our children grow into adulthood.

Still, this trip felt special. We were headed north from our home in Florida toward Canada, but we'd planned a special stop along the way. I'm an East Coast kid—I grew up in New Jersey. Traveling by RV would let us revisit my roots, spending time with one of my oldest friends, who had also been the best man at our wedding. This wasn't just a vacation but a chance to connect on multiple levels.

"How the hell..."

We pulled our rolling family sideshow into New Jersey just in time for Fourth of July celebrations. It was a beautiful weekend of barbecues, slow summer days, and great friends.

One afternoon, I struck up a conversation with a new acquaintance about my age. I'll call him Alex.

We stood together, two dads having a beer, watching kids scream and run in twenty different directions across the lawn. I pointed out ours (four of them at the time, now five). He pointed out his.

Then he pointed past the mayhem toward our RV in the distance.

"That yours?" Alex asked.

"We drove up from Florida," I said.

"Nice way to spend a week," he replied.

I opened my mouth—and then I closed it again.

The truth was we weren't out for a week. We'd *already* spent a week in the Outer Banks. From here, we were headed north into Maine, then on to Nova Scotia for another *month*. All told, we'd be gone for a good chunk of the summer.

I realized he was waiting for me to speak.

"This is week two of six," I admitted.

This time, he was the one who opened his mouth—and then closed it again. I could tell he was surprised, but in the beautiful chaos of a family picnic, we never finished our conversation.

I had forgotten the moment until I overheard Alex talking to my childhood friend the next day.

"What does that guy *do*?" Alex sounded incredulous. "How the hell can he take a six-*week* RV trip with his family?"

A wave of emotion moved through me. We had dedicated ourselves to building what we had come to call a *legendary family life*. His question validated so much of our approach, and I felt both grateful and proud.

But what I felt most was curiosity. Alex sounded almost *resentful*. But why? He was successful—a trip like ours wasn't financially out of reach. Yet here he was, asking *how do you do it all?*

That question would follow me from New Jersey north to Canada and then all the way back home again.

Eventually, it would lead to this book.

When Winning Becomes Losing

In our years of helping families build lasting bonds, we've met a lot of people like Alex. They share a set of characteristics:

• Through good luck and hard work, they've reached a level of financial comfort and professional success.

• The more success they find, however, the harder it seems to be to make time for the most important things in life—in particular, family relationships.

• Their efforts to change that, often through real estate or other seemingly passive investments, have failed to deliver or turned out to be second jobs.

• They've woken up to realize that life is *passing*. Their time with their kids—what we call *the 18 Summers*—is disappearing faster than they ever thought possible.

All of that is one scary combination—the stuff that wakes you up in the middle of the night, wondering *why does all this winning feel like losing*? It's a paradox that plagues almost everyone at a certain point.

At the heart of this winning/losing paradox is a sense that time and money are connected like a see-saw—more of one seems to leave less of the other.

•Make a great living for your family? *Sure. But you won't have time for them.*

•Make time for family adventure? *Sure. But you'll be broke.*

Alex, like so many people, was feeling that dilemma. Time and money in his world were inversely related. Our life, for him, didn't add up.

At some point during that RV trip, I realized that while I was incredibly proud of how we gave people the tools and strategies to put family first, we'd never *really* answered Alex's question.

How *did* we do it all?

This book is the answer.

Walking the Talk

My wife Jamie and I are best known as the authors of *The Family Board Meeting*. When the book landed at #1 on the Wall Street Journal bestseller list, it confirmed what we had heard for years:

successful entrepreneurs and busy professionals need a way to connect deeply with family before time runs out.

That book and our equally powerful way for spouses to connect (*Date Night With a Question*) form the core of what we call a *legendary family life*—a process and a set of values to deeply and permanently connect families. Some 300,000 people now use our simple tools and systems to create their own legendary family lives.

More important, I like to think we walk our talk. In just the last few years, I've:

•Taken several four-to-six-week family adventures to places around the world

•Donated a kidney to my father and provided the financial resources to help make it happen

•Helped retire my parents and provided a monthly stipend to support their lifestyle

•Helped start an alternative middle school for my sons to attend, including buying the building to house it

•Performed service work in three countries and supported several charities

•Wrote a bestselling book & created a family education company

•Helped hundreds of thousands of entrepreneurial families worldwide through our retreats and workshops

•Fostered two young children through the pandemic

•Lived in Costa Rica for four months annually

•Had a date night with my wife almost every week for many years

•Hit the beach almost every morning (I'm still surfing!)

What we've never done, however, is share how we *pay* for all of this.

The Three Challenges You're Facing

This book is for one very specific group of people: those who want the time and financial freedom to lead legendary family lives.

If that's you, then my guess is you're facing these three challenges:

1. You want to buy back your time. The most common sentiment I've heard from the many thousands of people we've spoken to is that *time has become scarcer than money.* You likely still see the value in your professional life, but your goals are changing. *You don't want to stop working. You want to stop missing out.*

2. You don't want *more* work. You need to disconnect time and money in your life in a way that doesn't feel like you're making things worse. *You don't want a second job. You want a second chance.*

3. You're interested in real estate but don't want to get burned (again). Anyone seeking passive income usually finds their way to real estate. But they often find their way to heartache, too. The reality television shows make it look easy, but it almost never is. *You don't need a reality show. You need a real solution.*

If those challenges resonate, then you've come to the right book.

The Road Ahead: How vs. How Much

I've never forgotten my conversation with Alex. It led to this book, but it also finally drove home for me the idea that our approach to financial and time abundance *works*. It really *is* possible to create wealth and remain deeply connected. It's possible to lead a legendary family life—one in which winning financially doesn't come at the cost of your health, happiness, and relationships.

But I also know that it takes *intention* and it takes a *plan*.

Our goal is to give you both of those.

We've learned (the hard way, as you'll see) that the secret to living a rich, connected life isn't what most people think it is.

Legendary family lives are built on *how* money is generated, not on how *much*.

If you feel like you've made a living for your family, but you're not quite sure if you're done making a *life*...then this book is for you.

To your legendary family life,

- Jim & Jamie

PART 1
The Power Of Passive

CHAPTER ONE

The First 2 Laws of Passive Income

W hy There Never Seems to Be Enough Time.

When I was a kid growing up in New Jersey, my mother kept a greeting card on the corner of her dresser. On the front, an attractive couple dressed in white walked the sand of a beautiful beach in the Virgin Islands.

My dad gave that card to my mom. Inside, he had written:

This will be us someday.
We'll travel to these places
and spend time together as a family.

The world, however, had other plans.

My dad worked hard. He was always the salesman. But he never seemed to catch a break. He sold electric typewriters—just as computers were on the rise. He worked commission sales—just as the recession hit. He started a business—just as the products went out of style.

Through it all, he struggled with money.

Over time, the card on my mom's dresser faded, and the dream did, too. We never took that trip to the Virgin Islands, spending most of the long winters in New Jersey instead. My parents never dressed in white linen or walked that beach.

It wasn't for lack of desire. My dad was a kind man, and I know he meant those words. I respected him deeply. What held him back was the lack of freedom and financial resources to bring the words to life.

I watched my father miss out, but I was determined to live the way that he only dreamed of. If we only get one shot at this life, I was going to live "someday" *today*.

But how?

My dad had always encouraged me to run my own business. To go my own way. But I'd watched him fail trying to do just that.

How was I going to avoid following in his footsteps?

The 5 Ways Real Estate Makes Money

I had learned that the three ways to become a millionaire were to own stocks, to own a business, or to own real estate. The more I read, the more people I spoke to, the more often real estate seemed to come up as the best of the three.

I had heard that 90% of millionaires made their money in real estate, and it seemed to crack the code I was trying to decipher. It was a way to run your own business like my dad suggested, but it also offered a way to live the life my parents never could.

Real estate, I was learning, made money in a lot of ways. Five of them, by my count:

1.Appreciation. Real estate was an asset that rose in value over time.

2.Leverage. Unlike most other assets, like stocks, you could buy a lot of real estate for very little money.

3.Debt paydown. Over time, someone else (a tenant) could pay off that real estate.

4.Tax benefits. Depreciation, interest deduction on debt, exchanges—there were a lot of tax advantages that were specific to real estate.

5.Cash flow. Real estate could put money in your pocket every month!

The previous year, I'd made about $24,000, and every dollar felt like a grind. The idea of more money—no matter how it arrived—seemed like a win to me. Five ways of making money just had to be better than one.

That's when the seeds of my real estate dream were planted. *If I could just buy one property,* I thought, *wouldn't that be something?*

Later that year, I found my opportunity. It was a triplex not far from where I lived. I knew the area well, but I was sweating buckets when I put in the offer. It was almost seven times my salary! I'd never seen that much money, never mind *spent* it. When the offer was accepted, I had a small moment of panic... then I dove in.

Almost right away, it was a huge success. And just like that, I was making money in real estate!

Naturally, my dream began to grow. What if I could buy *three* properties next year?

Three, of course, was a lot for a guy with no money. I began to look at foreclosures, which were a lot cheaper and the sellers more motivated.

I found someone to help finance the deals with just 10% down. I'd ask the seller to pay the closing costs and roll it all into the price and mortgage. That meant we'd only need to come up with a few thousand dollars to buy a house. We could buy a property, flip it, and make ten thousand dollars.

We bought three that year, just as I'd hoped.

I started to think, *what if I could buy one every month?*

And so on.

Flip...Flop

At that point, it was clear I was starting to make money. In the back of my mind was that greeting card on my mother's dresser. That unrealized dream. *I'm going to do it differently,* I thought.

And I was. But I was also working hard. Flipping was a grind. Over and over, I'd hustle to buy and sell a property. Then, I'd watch the new owner put tenants in the house and start collecting rent every month.

Wait a minute, I thought. All those flips I had done—where was that money? What did I have to show for it?

I looked back at the five ways real estate makes money. That's when it hit me: they only worked if you *held* the properties.

1.Appreciation. We weren't holding long enough for the market to rise. Any appreciation I got was from all the effort that went into the flip.

2.Leverage. We were leveraged, but flipping was uncertain. We were never sure if I'd gotten it right until we sold. Every ounce of leverage meant more stress.

3.Debt paydown. There was no tenant paying our mortgage—we were paying it out of pocket until we could get the property sold.

4.Tax benefits. Most tax advantages really only stacked up in the long run.

5.Cash flow. All of our properties were under renovation from day one. We had negative cash flow, and then we sold them for a one-time payout.

I couldn't believe it. Not only was I missing out on almost all the benefits of real estate, but every time I sold a house, I was starting over!

The Active Income Trap

Work, flip, repeat. I was making more money, yes, but I was grinding. I wasn't walking the beach any time soon.

Rehabbing and flipping houses, I was learning, was *active* income. It was another way to trade time for money. If I stopped hustling, stopped renovating, stopped looking for deals—the money stopped, too. All the money was coming from what was, in effect, a second job.

That moment was more than a lightbulb coming on. It was like a bucket of cold water. *This is why my dad never reached his dreams.* Even when he tried to make his own way, my father had been stuck in an active income *trap*. To make more money, he always needed more *time*.

And to make enough money to live out the dream on the card he'd given my mother? That would always take more time than he had.

If I followed my dad's path, there would *never* be enough time.

The Two Laws of Passive Income

Instead of active income, I realized I needed *passive* income. Passive income offered freedom through two key characteristics:

1.It takes very little effort. If you have to show up to get paid, it's not passive. If income requires ongoing work on your part, it's active income, not passive. Real estate typically generates passive income in the form of rental income.

2.It's predictable. Passive income is also *stable* income. If an income source varies wildly from month to month, two things happen. First, you start to worry about it. Second, you begin to work to maintain it. Worry and work are for *active* income, not passive. Real estate is an excellent way to build predictable cash flow.

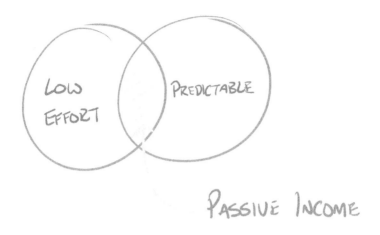

Passive income must meet two key criteria

As long as it didn't break those rules, income became *passive,* giving it a near-magical ability to disconnect time from money. It was a way to break out of the cycle my dad had always been stuck in.

Finally, I understood why every mentor had been telling me to *hold* real estate. Holding properties instead of selling them unlocked the full range of real estate benefits. It would give me income each month that required less effort *and* was more predictable than flipping.

I, of course, was doing the opposite.

My current real estate strategy took a lot of effort, *and* it was unpredictable. It was worse than a second job. If I changed my approach, I could not only replace the income from my job, but I could *count* on that money. It would come in whether I showed up at work or not.

That was the turning point. That was how I would live the way my dad had dreamed of. It was how I would get the beach, and the freedom, and the family time. True passive income was my ticket to a legendary family life.

The 100-House Mission

I now had a new mission. I was staying in real estate, but I was going to change my approach. Instead of flipping, we'd *hold* properties.

The first task was to learn how to be an investor, not a flipper. I was always keen to learn, and I loved to study how other people had become successful. I kept hearing about something called "The 100 House Club." *If you could get 100 properties*, the idea went, *you were set for life.* The passive income would pay your way, and over time, you'd become wealthy.

I became fixated on the idea. *Just get 100 houses. Just get 100 houses.* That was my mantra.

The trick, however, was that the market was becoming competitive. Buyers were showing up in my part of California from San Francisco and L.A. and bidding homes up to well over value. They were closing with no conditions. The high prices meant there was no cash flow. No cash flow meant no passive income.

At that rate, I'd either never get 100 houses, or they'd bankrupt me, so I started looking out of state.

Someone suggested northeast Florida. I'd always liked the East Coast. I grew up there, and we'd gone to Disney as a kid. I decided to check it out.

It was much better than California. Houses were cheap. To my 100-house mind, it was the promised land.

I got to work. One hundred houses, and I'd have all the passive income I needed. I'd bring my family to that beach, just like my dad had always promised. I was going to have a *legendary family life*.

What I didn't have was *context*.

No one told me that passive income was more complicated than it sounded in the books. And certainly, no one told me, "Hey, passive income can also destroy your life."

So I kept going. I was chasing those 100 houses. No matter what.

Then, the context arrived.

Chapter 1 Key Points

•Real estate makes money in five ways: *appreciation, leverage, debt paydown, tax benefits,* and *cash flow.*

•To access all those benefits, you need to *hold* properties, not flip them.

•Otherwise, real estate is *active* income, not *passive.* It's a second job.

•Passive income has two key characteristics: it takes *little effort* and is *predictable.*

•True passive income is what opens the door to a legendary family life.

CHAPTER TWO

The Third Law of Passive Income

How Passive Stays Passive

By 2007, I had well surpassed my 100-house goal.

I had left California feeling successful, but I arrived in Florida feeling like I'd found the land of real estate plenty! Here was a place with low prices, friendly tax and real estate laws, and effortless financing. My 100-house mission felt almost...easy.

Too easy, I now realize. The arrival of the subprime mortgage crisis made the flaw in my plan abundantly clear.

As the market tightened, money dried up, the economy began to buckle, and things began to fray. Property values were declining. People stopped paying rent because incomes were dropping. Refinancing became harder and harder. It was getting more and more difficult to maintain the business I'd built.

To stay afloat, I began selling some of the properties I still had in California. But values were dropping up to 60%. Rents were going down by 30%. I went from expecting checks every month to *writing* checks. I was paying money just to sell things!

Everything began to unravel. I was slowly, inexorably, losing it all.

By 2008, I was over three million dollars in debt. My net worth was deeply negative. I moved back in with my parents. That year, I paid myself $4000. For the *year*. That's how broke I was.

Later that same year, I wrote an entry in my journal: *Down to $78.04.*

Either something was going to change, or I was going bankrupt.

Back to the Grind

That was one of the hardest periods of my life. What made it harder was a single idea growing inside me: somehow, my drive to accumulate properties had *caused* this.

My 100-house dream had gone from being a boat surfing a rising tide to an anchor dragging me under. I knew that hard times are when the best lessons are learned, but I still didn't understand where I'd gone wrong. And I was too concerned with survival to figure it out.

The next five years were filled with a lot of pain.

I knew that the only way to stay alive was to keep doing deals. I had to *grow* my way out. While we held on for dear life to our properties and protected our investors, I started hustling.

The foreclosure market in Florida was growing in the wake of the subprime crisis, and I began buying foreclosed properties. Again.

Soon, I was buying ten to twelve foreclosures a month in partnership with brokers and private money. We'd close in a week for cash and renovate the homes.

This time, however, I'd learned my lesson. Instead of selling *all* the homes, we'd sell half of them and keep the other half to rent for passive income.

Even as I write this, I can see how it might sound great on paper. Buying a dozen remarkably cheap properties a month with 100% financing—who doesn't want that?

Anyone who wants to have a happy and stable life, that's who.

The Third Law of Passive Income

Buying all those inexpensive properties might sound sexy, but it was *hard*. I was dealing with problematic contractors. Unexpected costs. Difficult tenants. High turnover.

Eventually, I stabilized our financial life, but I realized I was heading right back down the "100 doors at any cost" road. My passive income was starting to feel very *active*. My phone rang almost constantly. There was a never-ending stream of issues to resolve. This didn't feel like the legendary family life I'd imagined.

I was still certain that real estate was the path to the life I wanted, but I knew something was wrong. There had to be a better way.

The problem, I realized, wasn't as simple as a mortgage crisis or a recession. The economy would always be out of my control. Somehow, this wasn't working.

To truly understand where things went wrong, I had to go back to the basics. Like *all* the way back.

I remembered the two laws that define passive income:

1. It takes little effort. (That's the *passive* part.)
2. It's predictable. (That's the *income* part.)

Break either of those rules, and passive income stops being passive. It either becomes active income, or it stops being income, *period*.

With that in mind, I went back and looked at all the hard parts of the crash through the passive income lens:

1. Why did my properties start taking so much effort?
2. Why did the income become unpredictable?

Problem by problem, house by house, I dug for answers. And problem by problem, house by house, the answers were always the same: *my properties sucked*.

It wasn't the most elegant discovery. And I didn't like the way it felt in my gut. But it was true.

I had bought a lot of bad properties in bad areas. I didn't realize it, but they were. When things started to get tough, those properties kicked off a cascade of problems:

•As the economy shut down, people stopped paying rent, and vacancies began to rise.

•Mortgages didn't care about the economy—there were still payments to make.

•Meanwhile, my cheap properties kept aging and needed more and more repairs.

•With less rent coming in, there was less money to cover those costs.

•As cash flow tightened, I had to do more and more work myself. Juggling all the demands of many properties became an ever-increasing part of my day.

In other words, my passive income fell apart. Eventually, what I had was *a second job that paid very poorly.* And I had only been making it worse by buying more foreclosures.

Not *all* of my properties were bad ones, mind you, and those told a different story. The few high-quality properties I had in good areas performed entirely differently:

•The tenants were less susceptible to sudden economic change. They continued to pay rent, and there were fewer vacancies.

•The properties were in better condition and needed less maintenance.

•The expenses I did have were more predictable. I knew exactly when the HVAC would need repairs or a roof would need replacing.

•The end result was that the income required less effort and remained more predictable.

Even in a recession, my higher-quality properties maintained their passive income and much of their value.

The real insight, I realized, was this:

The key to passive real estate income is *quality*.

Passive income, I realized, stopped being passive when it wasn't combined with *quality*. Passive income and quality were like conjoined twins. They need each other to survive and thrive. In all my education and study, no one had ever told me that **without quality, I would eventually break the first two laws of passive income.**

No quality meant:

•**Low-quality passive income eventually becomes *active* income.** Low-level buildings, tenants, and neighborhoods require high-level maintenance. They take more time, more money, and more peace of mind. Low-quality income is *active income*. And active income is another way of saying *job*. If you're like most successful people I know, another job is not what you're looking for.

•**Low-quality passive income eventually becomes unpredictable.** The low quality of the structures, tenants, and neighborhoods makes them less resilient to changes in the economy, changes in regulation, changes in climate, changes in *everything*. Every hiccup threatens the cash flow or increases expenses. At some point, low-quality income destabilizes and simply stops being income.

That's when I understood. *Quality was what unlocked passive income.*

The problem wasn't that I was in real estate.

It was that I was in the wrong *kind* of real estate.

The Three Quality Elements

I had learned that quality is what keeps passive income *passive*. How, I wondered, could I improve the quality of my properties and income?

I began to break down the problems I was having and realized they fell into three quality areas:

1. **Property.** The age and build quality of the home itself.

2. **Area.** The appeal and quality of the neighborhood the home was in.

3. **Tenant.** The stability and reliability of the people renting the home.

Every problem I had was related to one or more of those quality elements.

Those cheap properties meant my turnover and vacancy rates were higher. Rent payments were less predictable. There were more issues with property damage and complaints. Maintenance costs and hassles were higher.

My first thought was, "I can fix this." Surely, I could improve the homes or screen my tenants more diligently.

But the more I thought about those three problems, the more I realized they were *connected*.

On my quest for 100 houses, I had bought the cheapest homes I could afford.

•Cheap houses cost more to run.

•Cheap houses were often in less desirable neighborhoods.

•Cheap houses in bad areas attracted difficult tenants.

As long as I owned an eighty-year-old home, it was going to cost me more, no matter how much I worked on it. And I couldn't really change the neighborhoods. And that meant I couldn't attract different tenants.

Those three quality elements, I realized, formed a three-legged stool. As long as all three were present, a project could stand on its own three legs and deliver low-maintenance and reliable passive income.

But take away any single element, and passive income would falter.

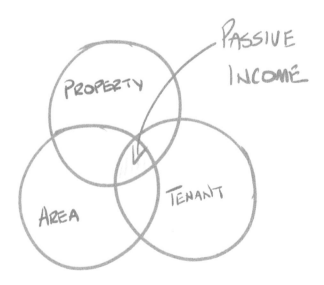

High-quality passive income happens when all three elements meet.

There was no way to solve just one problem. I needed to solve *all* the problems.

An Idea!

That was the lightbulb moment.

If I wanted true *passive* income—income that was both low-effort *and* stable—I needed to attach it to quality. That was how I'd build an income that gave me both the time *and* the financial resources to lead a legendary family life.

But if I truly wanted *quality*—in property, area, and tenant—then I couldn't keep focusing on old fixer-uppers. I needed something better.

From that moment on, when I wasn't living the nightmare of terrible properties in terrible areas, I was dreaming of better ones. I imagined having a *new* property. No surprises. Predictable maintenance. High-quality tenants who stayed for years. Modern materials and modern building standards. Energy efficiency. The list went on.

The more I lived out the drama of owning old homes, the more I began to dream of new ones.

Imagine, I thought, *building something specifically for renting.* Not buying some old home and converting it, but *starting the way we intended to finish.* Purpose-built. High quality. Appealing homes in appealing areas.

I had a building partner that we'd been working on and off with for a few years—we'd sold them a few properties or vice versa. But we'd never really built anything together. One day, he came to me with an idea.

What if we built our own?

Chapter 2 Key Points

• Passive income only stays passive if it's connected to *quality*.

• Quality in real estate has three elements: *property*, *area*, and *tenant*.

• The highest quality passive income is generated where all three elements meet.

• The best way to guarantee all three elements is in new construction.

CHAPTER THREE

The Power of New

Real Estate 2.0 and the Build-To-Rent Revolution

It's not as if I had never thought of building something new.

Trust me, when you own lousy properties, you dream of shiny new buildings with perfect plumbing, flawless wiring, and roofs that don't leak. You fantasize about unpluggable toilets and rooms where the walls actually meet at right angles.

Until now, however, that had been nothing more than fantasy. Buying cheap properties was what I knew. Price was my big motivation.

Now, I felt like I was seeing things through a new lens. Instead of simply seeing quality as "better buildings," I began to see new construction as a better *investment*. New construction, I realized, could solve the quality issue at all three levels.

- We could build new with materials and skills we trusted.
- We could choose the neighborhoods we built in.
- We could attract great tenants who wanted a long-term relationship.

That, in turn, solved the real problem: creating *true* passive income. Income that was both low effort *and* reliable.

That would let me create the legendary family life that my father had wanted but never found.

Real Estate 2.0

I was also starting to suspect that new construction might solve another challenge.

By 2015, most of the foreclosure inventory—all the homes that had been lost in the 2008 crash—had been bought. We still wanted to keep growing, but we were struggling to find properties. When I spoke to other investors, the story was the same. Deals were getting harder to come by. Each dollar was buying less house and less rental income.

But I felt there was something deeper at work. For a long time, real estate was a way of investing reserved for the risk-takers and the wealthy. It had always been a powerful tool, but like stocks, it hadn't always been popular. When I started out, there were no TV shows or influencers teaching the world to buy rental homes.

Now, it seemed like everyone wanted to be a flipper or a landlord. Things were simply more competitive. What had, at first, felt like an economic problem was starting to seem like more of a seismic shift.

I began to think of this as a new playing field. It was "Real Estate 2.0," and it was defined by a new set of rules:

•**More capital than properties.** There were a lot of buyers with a lot of money chasing fewer homes. That was driving prices up.

•**Smaller cash flows.** Paying more for properties meant margins were down. Returns were lower.

•**Unpredictable conditions.** Housing legislation, economic shifts, and interest rates were all unknown factors. Uncertainty wasn't new in real estate, but with smaller margins and higher prices, those risks were harder to manage.

When I looked at those changes, I started to see how building new properties could help. Building from scratch meant we were creating our *own* supply and would not be as subject to supply issues. We could also pick states that were landlord-friendly and areas that were attractive to great tenants. We could create well-built homes with predictable costs. And in Florida, where we were focused, we could build homes that were incredibly hurricane-resistant. We could choose higher ground, and build to higher standards. (A strategy that would be successful tested before long!)

We could, I realized, even control interest rates to an extent by developing in-house financing with rates up to 2% lower than most mortgage companies.

In Real Estate 2.0, we could control *quality* at every level. And that meant we could control passive income.

Yeah, but...

Despite *all* those reasons to try things differently, I was skeptical.

Actually, I was more than skeptical—I was completely against the idea! It seems crazy in hindsight, but at the time, I thought it was just too expensive to build. I was still in the "get it cheap" mindset.

Development fees, for example—charges by a municipality for new construction—felt like throwing away money. "Why would we do that?" I argued. "Let's get a place that someone else has already paid those fees on. Plus, do you know how expensive new materials are?"

I was using the same philosophy you might use to buy a car: find a used one that someone has already taken the hit on.

But that was the wrong philosophy. When you're trying to build a *fleet* of cars, you don't want a whole pile of crappy old sedans—you want quality you can build a business on. When you're trying to build passive real estate income, you don't want crappy old properties—you want quality you can build a *life* on.

I should have realized that sooner. Instead, I just saw new construction as too expensive.

Fortunately, I was dead wrong.

Time to Build

Eventually, I agreed that we should build one rental property from scratch. The allure of a shiny new, well-built home was too attractive not to try.

So we did it.

And—it didn't go that well.

The costs ran higher than expected. We were used to patching up fixer-uppers with glue and string, not building a quality duplex from scratch. We also made some bad choices with tenants. We were used to renting older homes to less-than-ideal customers, not choosing long-term relationships carefully.

Still, we could see this build-from-scratch thing had legs.

I knew if we could scale—do more—we could get good at all the parts beyond just building. We could create systems for tenants and maintenance and rent and all the other details of property management.

Moreover, I thought we could fix the numbers. If we were building a *lot* of homes, we could buy windows by the thousands instead of by the dozen. We'd save a pile of money on material costs. If we built houses the same, we'd be able to do more, faster, less expensively, and get the same or better quality.

Doing all of that, of course, meant building a lot more homes. And building a lot more meant we needed cash. We decided to start selling off the painful, low-quality properties and using the proceeds to fund new construction.

The Build-to-Rent Revolution

We didn't invent the idea of building new rental units, of course. People have always built apartment buildings and other multi-family properties.

But we weren't the only people discovering the Real Estate 2.0 shift.

In the wake the Great Recession, foreclosures had skyrocketed. Private and institutional investors could, perhaps for the first time, buy residential homes at scale. From around 2010, investors bought nearly a quarter of a million single-family homes and turned them into rentals.

As the supply of homes tightened, large investors went through the same process as we did, eventually realizing that rather than picking over old properties that needed work, they could *build* properties. Some chose to build entire *communities* of build-to-rent homes and get the benefit of scale.

Soon, a new category was born, Build-To-Rent (BTR), defined loosely by:

•Choosing single-family homes, duplexes, or other designs with ground-level access

•Designing smaller, median-sized homes to fill a growing need in the market

•Building homes in carefully selected communities to create a healthy balance of owners and renters

•Constructing at scale when possible, buying numerous infill lots in great communities, or even building entire developments

By 2020, the BTR market had some of the lowest vacancy rates in the industry, and was a legitimate asset class in its own right.[1]

The Benefits of a Targeted BTR Approach

• **Stable valuations.** We build median-sized properties—typically 1400 square feet or less. They not only fill an enormous demand in the market, but median properties tend to hold their value better during market changes. We used to protect ourselves by buying cheap properties on sale. For years, I thought I was building a moat of safety. Instead, it almost sank me. Now, our safety moat is high-quality construction around the median.

•**More predictable expenses.** In tough times, the maintenance costs on older properties killed our cash flow. It always seemed like those properties were cash cows at first. But when the market is going sideways, and you're paying out of pocket or taking on debt to replace a roof, etc., things can go badly very quickly. Building and buying quality stabilizes cash flows more predictably. You get fewer surprises in tough times. You can prepare for future maintenance with a high level of confidence.

•**More stable income.** Median-sized, high-quality homes support stable tenants who pay rent consistently. Lower quality has high turnover, and tenants are less likely to pay rent in tough times. Higher-end properties are often short-term rentals or vacation properties—they're optional, and vacancies skyrocket during market cycles.

• **More appreciation in the good times.** Median properties are also known for appreciating well when the market is strong. That means you build even *more* safety during the good times, which gives you more cushion in a downturn.

•**Fewer headaches.** Quality construction, great tenants, and excellent locations make property management a dream. There are fewer surprises. People are happier. Everyone involved—from the tenants to the investors to the management team—sleeps a lot better at night.

What do you get when you combine all those benefits? *True passive income.* Income that takes little effort *and* is predictable.

That lets us focus on the *why* behind the passive income—building a legendary family life.

Burning Bridges and Build-to-Rent

When we decided to try our first build-to-rent experiment, we owned about 180 properties. I had blown past my 100-house goal and was all in on real estate.

Most of those properties were low quality, and that cost me dearly—in time, money, and peace of mind. It nearly sank us.

Since then, my entire real estate philosophy has shifted. The year after that first experimental BTR, we did 60 brand-new properties built specifically to rent—mostly smaller, single-family homes, the odd duplex, or quad.

The following year, we did 260.

And everything has changed.

Our new approach not only fits a new Real Estate 2.0 world, but it also fits *us*. It lets us focus on our family and our values. For us, that's what matters most.

The philosophy is as simple as it is powerful:

Own less real estate of higher quality.

We now:

•Choose quality over quantity
•Own fewer homes but in better areas
•Choose more life, less leverage

It's a philosophy that fits us. But it's also a philosophy that I can, with an open heart and clear conscience, recommend to anyone, from a stranger at a party to my own family.

Since that first BTR house, we now own 80% *fewer* properties. And we have more equity and more cash flow than ever.

That cash flow is *passive* in the true sense of the word. By focusing on quality at every level, the income is both low-effort and very reliable.

It's that income that powers our family and allows us to live in alignment with our values. I feel like I'm finally living the life my dad dreamed of.

We have now "burned our bridges" in terms of older, lower-quality properties. We only do new construction. Good areas. Great tenants. Excellent homes. We are known as the BTR people, building quality houses that great families can afford to rent.

And we couldn't be happier.

After twenty years, I've come to a place where I know *there's a new way to do things*. A better way. But that journey has also taught me there's a *wrong* way to do things, too.

In Part II, we're going to look at both—the keys to success in BTR but also the pitfalls.

Chapter 3 Key Points

•Real estate as an investment has become more popular and more competitive.

•The new real estate playing field is defined by higher prices, lower returns, and higher risk.

•Build-to-rent helps in this new environment by offering more stable valuations, predictable expenses, steady income, greater appreciation in uncertain times, and fewer headaches.

PART 2
Build-To-Rent

CHAPTER FOUR
The 5 Success Indicators

Finding the Best Market for Your BTR Investment

Adam Hamilton grew up in Virginia, the son of a steel-worker, in a family where money was a challenge. "We never owned our primary residence," he recalled. "My parents just did everything wrong financially."

His grandfather owned a farm, and that became the work Adam knew best. Yet, while it earned him some cash, his biggest lesson was, in his words, "There's gotta be a better way."

Adam wasn't sure what that way *was*, but after heading west to college, he decided some kind of financial sales would pay best. If nothing else, a good income would substitute for the financial education he never had at home.

He eventually landed in the mortgage business, which exposed him for the first time to the world of real estate ownership. "Pretty quickly, I knew that I wanted to own some kind of rental real estate," he said, "but I didn't have any mentors or understanding of it. It took me a while before I even bought my first home."

Still, by age 27, Adam and his wife had purchased a house in Salt Lake City, Utah. Adam told her that one day, it would become their first rental property.

When they bought a new home, that vision came to life. Although it didn't make a lot of money, that first rental put Adam in the real estate business. He was on his way.

The arrival of the mortgage crisis was stressful, but for Adam, it also felt like an opportunity to expand. Despite trying times for the mortgage industry, he set a goal to buy five more properties in the Salt Lake City area.

Eventually, Adam found his five properties in Salt Lake. But he also found himself at a crossroads based on two challenges:

1. As mortgage rates dropped in the years following the crash, home prices began to rise in the Salt Lake area. It got harder and harder to make the numbers work as an investor.

2. Adam was self-managing his properties while working a demanding full-time job. Even if he could find homes to buy, there was no breathing space left in his schedule to manage them.

Adam was beginning to see the first cracks appear in his passive income strategy. What he didn't realize at the time was that he'd just bumped up against two problems that build-to-rent was perfectly poised to solve.

Where, oh, Where?

Let's take a step back and recap our journey so far:

•Passive income, defined by low effort and high predictability, is a powerful way to create more time and energy for your most important relationships.

•One of the most effective tools in history for creating passive income is real estate.

•*But*...real estate can also do the opposite. The wrong kind of real estate can destroy passive income.

•The key lies in *quality* properties. Without quality, passive income eventually fails.

•There are three quality factors in real estate: *building*, *tenant*, and *location*.

Of the three quality factors that determine passive real estate income, location is one that is most overlooked. (Ironic, given the old saying *location, location, location.*)

There is no way to fix a bad neighborhood with a nicer building or better tenants. The right location is the bedrock on which all real estate income is built.

The question now is, *what determines the best location?* We know we're going to build a new, quality income property. That will enable us to attract great tenants. Those two things alone will *almost* ensure our passive income. But where should we build it?

We use five success indicators to help choose locations and new markets:

1. Economic Growth
2. Population Growth
3. Affordability
4. Desirability
5. Supply & Demand

Each one contributes to location quality. Location quality, in turn, contributes to the five ways in which real estate makes money—including making sure that your passive income stays passive. Find a market with all five of the success indicators, and, as an investor, you'll have the wind at your back.

In Salt Lake, Adam was facing a location problem. To grow, he needed to find a new market that fit all five success indicators. Let's look at each in turn.

Success Indicator #1: Economic Growth

Economic growth in a market means, in a word, *jobs*. Good employment means stable tenants who can care for properties and pay rent reliably. That, in turn, means quality passive income.

To find markets with solid economic growth, we research and track job-related factors like employment levels, industry types, and median family income.

Anywhere you see economic growth, you'll also see growth in the next success indicator...

Success Indicator #2: Population Growth

Between January 2012 and June 2021, some 12.3 million American households were formed. Each one of those households, by definition, needs a "house"—an address.

We also know that the U.S. population grew by about 20 million people over the same time period.

Those numbers both point to growth—and that's a good thing if you're in the business of building homes. But when we're trying to answer the question of *where* to focus your build-to-rent efforts, we need to know which *states* all of those people are moving to. Population growth numbers by state are readily available—look for states with rising levels.

Success Indicator #3: Affordability

In the United States, not enough homes are being built, and those that are being built are not the *right* homes. Since 2008, the number of newly built homes under 1,400 square feet has declined to about 8% of builds.[2] Zoning is making small homes more difficult to build, and many builders simply don't *want* to build smaller homes.

We focus our BTR efforts on areas where we can build *median-sized* homes. They're always in demand, but they need to be affordable. Home affordability numbers are easy to find online by state and by metropolitan area, and they are one of our most important criteria. If the average family can't afford the average house, it's an uphill battle for everyone, including BTR investors.

Success Indicator #4: Desirability

Sometimes, you find an area that meets the first three indicators—economic growth, population growth, and affordability—but you also find the area simply isn't that attractive. It may be that amenities haven't caught up with the growth or the growth, itself, is causing additional challenges.

We always look for areas that have some combination of desirable characteristics, including:

- Lifestyle factors like walkability and recreation
- Natural appeal like beaches, forests, water, and weather
- Lower crime
- Better schools
- A mix of homeowners and renters
- For our investors, landlord-friendly laws and regulations

A growing, affordable area that's also desirable? That's a place to put down a foundation.

Success Indicator #5: Supply and Demand

The first four success indicators point to one thing: a demand for homes in a particular area. If an area is thriving, growing, affordable, and desirable, there will be demand. No question.

In isolation, all that demand might seem like a recipe for build-to-rent success.

But demand never exists in a vacuum. Demand's twin is *supply*. We might find an excellent BTR area, but if there are already a number of permits out and homes in construction, that may be enough to meet the demand.

In other words, we're looking for a place where we can build supply to meet rising demand.

Fortunately for BTR investors, household formation is out-pacing homebuilding. What does that mean for you, the investor? When demand for a product is greater than its supply, the price rises. We are *millions* of homes short in the United States—especially in hub markets like Florida. That's like a blinking neon sign saying *Investors Wanted!*

The Sweet Spot

What we're trying to find, then, is where all five success indicators *overlap:*

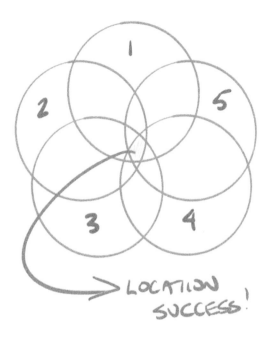

The best BTR meets all 5 success indicators

Do you have to hit *all* the success indicators? Not necessarily. Just remember that anytime you miss one, you risk the quality of your passive income. The more boxes you tick, the closer you get to guaranteed success.

Meeting all five success indicators might seem like a tall order, but it's more than possible. We've done it over and over. The "secret" is to escape the mindset of the typical real estate investor. That was something Adam was on his way to uncovering.

Out of Your Comfort Zone

Not every market works.

In fact, *most* of them don't. The odds of your local area meeting the five criteria are relatively small. Like many of our clients, you may be discovering you can't make real estate work in your backyard anymore.

Adam had found that Salt Lake City was no longer hitting all five success indicators. Or, to put it another way, Salt Lake had become so attractive to other investors and home buyers that it had become...unattractive. This is a common challenge for investors, and often what brings them to us. Many of our out-of-state and international investors are finding properties are priced at a *third* of what they are in their home markets. (See the Appendix for more international BTR insights.)

To grow his passive income and freedom, Adam had to do something that most real estate investors shy away from: he had to leave the comfort of his home state.

One of the greatest barriers to hitting all five BTR success indicators isn't *finding* a market that meets them all—those markets are out there. The challenge is opening your mind to the idea of investing out-of-state.

To create *quality* passive income, you may need to leave the perceived safety of your home base. There are two main ways to do this:

•**DIY.** You absolutely can do this all yourself. Find a good out-of-state market, and buy *excellent quality* real estate, or have it built for you. Hire property management to run it.

•**Partner.** Find a BTR developer that you can trust to manage the entire process, from finding the right location to building the home, then finding the tenants and managing the property.

Adam, in fact, did a little of both.

His out-of-state exploration eventually led him to Florida. It met all five success indicators and added a bonus for his family: he could combine a great vacation with a chance to visit income properties. "Detroit was another area I looked into," Adam said, "but I didn't want to go to Detroit for vacation."

That same exploration also led him to build-to-rent. "It was kind of new at the time, and I was intrigued by it," he recalled.

After settling in Florida, Adam went on to buy some existing properties but then moved steadily into build-to-rent.

Five Indicators=One Passive Income Success

When we spoke to Adam, he had just set up a new tenant in one of his older existing rentals in Salt Lake City.

"I probably put fifteen hours of time into setting up a listing and getting tenants in. Of course, the first three days, they're also finding all the problems in the house that I still need to fix."

Adam's older homes continue to take more time to manage than he would like.

His build-to-rent properties, however, are an entirely different story. They pass both tests of passive income with flying colors. "I bet I spend an hour a month," he said, "and that is just checking to be sure I got paid. I don't even have to do that every month."

The five success indicators aren't complicated. It's executing on them that's hard. It takes time and effort to properly analyze a market. And it takes a little extra courage to go outside your home state.

Our argument has always been simple: *your family is worth the effort*. The payback for looking harder, further, and more deliberately for the *right* place to invest is passive income you can rely on—income that delivers time and financial abundance so you can focus on what matters most.

As Adam said, "I give the same advice all the time to people. You can be afraid of going out of state, but I'm more afraid of buying a rental that doesn't cash flow."

Choosing the right market isn't the only thing you need to get right. Once you find the sweet spot where all five success indicators overlap, you'll need to avoid a few landmines on the way to creating your build-to-rent investment future.

Chapter 4 Key Points

•Of the three quality factors that determine passive real estate income, location is the most overlooked.

•Location quality is determined by five success indicators: economic growth, population growth, affordability, desirability, and supply & demand.

•To meet all five success indicators, you may need to leave the comfort zone of your home state.

CHAPTER FIVE

The 5 Traps

Where BTR Goes Wrong

Two years into our first build-to-rent efforts, I had finally come to understand the connection between real estate and relationships.

I knew that quality real estate created true passive income. True passive income, in turn, was the base for the *legendary family life* I wanted.

Still, life was far from perfect. Intellectually, it all made sense, but in my heart, habits, and mindset, I still had some growing to do.

I had spent the previous seven years looking over my shoulder, always weeks away from running out of money, weeks away from financial disaster. I was running, always running. My phone rang constantly. Every time I solved one problem, two more would spring up.

Things were so hard in those early days of BTR that I felt like our legendary family life might be in jeopardy. I knew that our life was suffering a slow death by a thousand cuts, and I knew it had to stop. But I had gotten myself into a difficult spot (number five on the list that follows).

And I wasn't sure how to get out.

The Five Traps

Many people have a real estate story that echoes the problems I faced. The story goes like this: *I wanted to build wealth. I was told real estate was the tool for the job. But I tried it, and it was a nightmare. I'm out. Never again.*

If that feels like your story, you have almost certainly fallen into at least one of the five traps that follow.

These pitfalls aren't specific to build-to-rent. Done right, BTR is designed to help *avoid* them. But make no mistake, you can fall into them just the same. And I can tell you from experience it's *far* easier to avoid them than to get out of them!

The five traps are:

1. Short-term thinking
2. Do-it-yourself
3. Chasing cheap
4. Misdirected charity
5. Wrong partners

Let's look at each in turn.

Trap #1: Short-Term Thinking

A few years ago, I traveled to Ireland to uncover my roots. I come from an Irish Catholic family, and that means big families and deep roots!

The trip was a revelation. I stood at my great-grandmother's grave. I sat with my oldest living relative, who had over 200 years' worth of letters, documents, and photos of my family history. I saw the source of my entrepreneurial spirit in my great-grandfather's little Irish country store.

That trip, and the self-insight that came with it, was made possible by our real estate investments.

What surprised me most, however, was what I learned about real estate itself. In Ireland, I saw the house my great-grandfather and grandfather grew up in. He had the house built for a few hundred dollars almost 150 years ago, and *it's still in the family*. It's gone from Sheils to Sheils to Sheils to Sheils. From Michael to Eddie to Oliver to Michael. My second cousin still owns it. That's a 142-year buy-and-hold!

I think we all feel the allure of the short-term win. But standing in Ireland in front of a century and a half of history in one house—that was the most powerful long-term symbol I'd ever seen. My early days of flipping took timing, risk, and struggle. Here was an incredible win for my family, and all it took was the passage of time.

If you bought an investment property the day before the crash in 2007, you would have bought on what arguably was the worst day to buy in the last century.

And yet, by simply holding the property, *you'd have more than doubled your money by now.* Plus, you'd have the tax advantages, debt reduction, and cash flow while you waited!

Many people still try to play the old Real Estate 1.0 game. They buy the cheapest property they can find so they can make money tomorrow instead of investing in quality that lasts and generates true passive income for the long run.

The longer you hold good properties, the better and better things get. Your luck gets better. Your safety margins get bigger. Your wealth grows. Short-term is just the opposite.

Like my Irish ancestors, we avoid the short-term thinking trap. We plant seeds for the long term so that we can harvest for generations.

Trap #2. Do-It-Yourself

An investor friend recounted to me how repairs on his first property almost drove him out of real estate for good.

"The water meter under the house froze in the middle of winter and began flooding the crawl space," he recalled. "I lay on my back in a pool of slush, ice-cold water spraying over me, trying to repair it. Within a few minutes, I was so cold I lost all the feeling in my arms and legs and could barely crawl back out."

The worst part, he said, is that he was doing it to avoid paying an available plumber. "I could have stayed warm and dry—and got the job done properly—with one phone call."

It got worse.

"Seven months later," he said, "I was lying in the same crawl space, this time in raw sewage, trying to replace more plumbing. All to save a few bucks."

Nothing drives people out of real estate faster than DIY.

The phone calls during family vacations. The weekends spent pouring your time and energy into old buildings. The time spent finding great tenants—and the even *greater* time spent getting rid of bad ones and recovering afterward.

If you're trying to focus on family, you don't want any of that. You don't want the job of checking credit. Doing renos. Answering the phone. Fixing plumbing in the middle of winter—or summer.

Almost every real estate investor reaches a point where self-managing their properties no longer makes sense—not for them, their tenants, and certainly not their families.

My friend learned that the hard way. "Now," he told me, "the only tool I'm allowed to use is my phone."

Trap #3: Chasing Cheap

I spent years looking for inexpensive properties that I could buy for as little money as possible. And let me tell you: when you're good at finding deals, and you really focus on finding cheap places, they are out there.

There are places so cheap you don't even need a loan. The return seems amazing. Cheap houses cash flow like crazy...on paper. In reality, I discovered many of those houses were almost as flimsy as *actual* paper.

It's the greatest "scam" in real estate. It's a simple pitch: Buy low, make easy money. If it sounds too good to be true, it's because it is. When the mortgage crisis arrived, I was suddenly an overwhelmed small fish in a very big and expensive pond.

It took me over a decade to get out of those bad properties. Let me make sure that sinks in: *it took me from the 2008 crash until the 2020 pandemic to undo all the painful real estate investments I'd made by chasing cheap.*

With the benefit of hindsight, I can now see what *all* of my painful lessons in passive income had in common: they were low-quality properties in bad areas. I was buying as much cheap as I could afford.

It should have come as no surprise. Chasing cheap *always* leads to a sacrifice in one or more of the three quality elements of location, property, or tenant. It can lead you to states that aren't landlord-friendly, to poorly built homes, or to tenants that are hard to form long-term relationships with. And they will all take from your family in some way.

Cheap is cheap for a reason.

Trap #4. Misdirected Charity

When I first made the transition from flipping homes to actually holding them and renting them, I was doing almost everything myself. That included screening tenants—a task I had no experience in. I was just making it up as I went along!

With the first four of five tenants, I began to hear excuses—stories about why the rent was late, or only half paid, or not paid at all. I always wanted to see the best in people, and I found it hard not to get drawn into the drama. I found myself getting too emotionally close. I started letting people get behind. Eventually, half of my small portfolio wasn't paying rent! It put my business at risk, and I didn't have the deep pockets to support it.

We'd try to create great spaces for people who we thought needed help. But in the end, it never worked. The help never seemed to...help. Inevitably, even the tenants ended up worse off for our efforts.

It was charity, with none of the good feelings. It was the most disheartening form of charity I've ever experienced, and worse still, it interfered with us giving to the causes we most cared about.

Instead, we focus on generating quality passive first and then using that income to give back.

Trap #5. Wrong Partners

I like to think that most things in life are lessons.

The tough times I have had in real estate were also learning opportunities. That's where I gained wisdom. We wouldn't be where we are today without those moments, and given the chance, I wouldn't change them.

There is one exception.

I've had partners for almost all of my journey—Jamie being the most important. I have always felt that allowing people to live in their core genius, to focus on what they do best, is a powerful way to operate. And that takes partnerships. High-quality passive income, I've discovered, is a team sport.

But partnerships aren't always easy. After a number of years together, I wanted to separate from my business partner at the time. The relationship had become toxic and unproductive, and I knew our partnership had run its course. My mentor even flew in to spend a day figuring out how to do it.

Yet I was in that partnership for more than a dozen more years before I finally ended it.

If there is one thing I'd change, given the chance, it would be to have separated when I first recognized the problem. I know now just how important it is to choose the right partners, to deal with them with integrity, and to make sure that your values are aligned. A business partner isn't that different from a life partner in that way—you need to have a similar moral compass. You need to share both beliefs and a *why* that powers your life. It was Jamie who finally taught me that lesson, and given the chance, I'd take her and that lesson back in time with me.

Now, we no longer actively pursue opportunities with investors—*we pursue relationships with people who resonate with our values.* We look for people who want to prosper for the same reason we do—to create legendary family lives. That keeps us on the same page. It keeps us all in our core genius, doing what we do best and spending our time in the way that matters most. And it's why 75% of our clients never see their properties in person. They simply don't *need* to because they've chosen the right partner.

Success isn't a lottery where you just keep buying random tickets and hope to win. Success is about making the best choices. Good things have come out of my bad partnership choices, but we certainly could have found good things without those mistakes. Better not to have made them in the first place.

Price of Everything, Value of Nothing

If you're like me, then you have an eye for *opportunity*. You're seeking value out there in the world. Although we've "burned our bridge" to Real Estate 1.0, I can't deny there is still the occasional temptation to go back to the old ways. To buy that "great deal" on the fixer-upper.

What I've learned is that value and price are *not* the same thing. Not even close. And at times, they're opposites.

The five traps are guardrails to keep you pointed toward *value*. Toward what is truly important in investing. And in doing so, they help point you toward what is important in *life*.

I'm still tempted to go to the office and work long hours because that's the model I was taught. I was told that was how you create *value*. But I realized that wasn't true. Anyone who has found some success in life has reached a point where they *can't* create more value by grinding. If you've already found some success, then grinding is a *price*. Grinding is buying a cheap house in a lousy neighborhood. Or thinking short-term. Or doing everything yourself. It's being seduced by a story that no longer fits the place you've reached in life.

It's time to stop shopping based on the price tags in life. It's time to start seeing your life through the lens of *value*.

Each trap can be reframed as a *choice*—a decision to change the way you approach BTR:

1.Think long-term. Remember, you're creating quality passive and *long-term* income to support a legendary family life.

2.Delegate. Don't waste time doing things that you aren't good at and don't enjoy. Don't sacrifice family time to save money. Leverage the remarkable skills and passions of other people.

3.Choose value over price. Cheap isn't cheap. Cheap is putting off the real price until later when your family will have to pay it in lost time and connection.

4.Let your business fund your charity. Don't let it *be* your charity.

5.Choose relationships based on values. Seek relationships for *life*, not to try to turn a quick buck now.

When you choose wisely, you live a life outside the traps.

Chapter 5 Key Points

•Like any real estate investment, BTR has pitfalls to avoid. There are five significant traps: short-term thinking, do-it-yourself, chasing cheap, misdirected charity, and wrong partners.

•Each trap can be repositioned as a rule for BTR success:

1. Think long-term.
2. Delegate.
3. Choose value over price.
4. Let your business fund your charity.
5. Choose relationships based on values.

CHAPTER SIX

The BTR Storyline

The Journey from Build...to Rent

When I first got into real estate, the formula seemed simple: you find a house, you fix it up, you sell it.

I soon discovered the very real downside to that formula. It was simple, but it didn't lead to quality passive income. That, in turn, didn't support a legendary family life.

When we started building new homes for rent, I still had that simple approach in mind. I thought, "Let's get a piece of land, put a house on it, and rent it." In my mind, it was still a three-step process: Buy. Build. Rent.

Boy, did I get an education.

I had *no* idea of the skills, finesse, and expertise it takes to do BTR right, to do it at scale, and to do it in a way that would make nearly a thousand investors happy!

I've since learned from people who do know. Many homes and many happy tenants and investors later, I can do a *much* better job of explaining the process of how a BTR idea becomes a happy family living in a great home backed by delighted investors.

The seven-step process that follows took us years to refine, but we can now replicate it in multiple locations and economic markets, for investors who want true passive income.

Step #1: Acquire

One truism in BTR—and a lot of real estate—is that *you make your money when you buy the land*. That's our shorthand for remembering that careful selection and negotiation early on create great returns for our clients. And it's why every BTR project starts with an acquisition strategy.

In our experience, most properties on the market are overpriced. If you're trying to build in a way that serves tenants but also creates a rental yield for investors, those public deals put you at a disadvantage right away.

Our solution is to find property that's *not* listed. We have a dedicated team that scours GIS maps and public records. Their job is to look for specifically sized parcels in our target areas (based on the principles in Chapter 4).

When we find vacant parcels that meet our requirements, we track down the owners. That information is then passed to our Negotiation Team. They're the ones who connect with the actual landowners to discuss:

- If they're willing to sell the land
- At what price
- How much time we can have to evaluate the property (Step #2)

Generally, building a house costs the same regardless of how much we pay for the land. The way we create value and generate better returns is to do the hard work necessary to find great deals on the land itself.

When we do that, it doesn't mean we've purchased the property. It means we have it *under contract*—we have an option to purchase it. But before we do that, we need to dig in for some next-level due diligence.

Step #2: Evaluate

Building a house may seem complicated. But construction is relatively straightforward compared to the challenge of trying to decide *if we should even build the house at all.*

After we get a property under contract, we start an in-depth due diligence process. This is where I truly discovered how much care and expertise is invested before money changes hands or shovels hit the ground. In this phase, we look at hundreds of details, including:

- Property zoning and requirements for rezoning
- Infrastructure requirements for water, sewer, retention ponds, lift stations, and power
- Natural challenges like floodplains, wetlands, sinkholes, or protected habitat/species
- Archeological or other important/protected cultural concerns
- Toxic chemicals, gas tanks, or other previous industrial uses

•The number of lots that can be realistically created

•Financing implications, project timelines, and access to capital

During this long phase, we work with local government and zoning commissions, meet with community members, take soil samples, explore the property, and work with experts in every field, from environmental protection to civil engineering.

All this time, the property owner still owns the land and waits patiently for us to complete our due diligence. It's why we look for landowners who see us as *partners*. They have the land, and we're the experts who can analyze every detail to get the property ready for a single home—or an entire community.

Sometimes, we discover we can buy the property at an attractive price, but it will cost an enormous amount to rezone it and deal with infrastructure. In those cases, the property may become too expensive before we build a single home. In some developments, we've spent millions of dollars to do everything from building enormous lift stations for water to creating cypress gardens and protecting tortoises!

When the numbers work and everything lines up, we can move to the next step: Purchase.

Step #3: Purchase

When we're building an entire community, after a period of many months, we'll have created a *plan*. It takes into account everything from zoning to roads to water to sewer to open space. That plan—in essence, a series of very detailed, very expensive engineering drawings—is sent to the municipality. After some back and forth, we get the official stamp of approval on the development. After all that work, it's time to actually *buy* the land!

This usually happens within about fifteen days. We do another title search, then close on the property. Money changes hands, title changes hands, and we're almost ready to start development.

During the brief period between approved plans and closing, we're able to take another important step. Our Development Services Team has already done their own estimate of what it will cost to build the community. Now, they send the approved plans out to a series of site contractors.

Those vendors come back with their own scope of work and pricing. We can then make sure their numbers line up and that the contractor has the right resources and experience for the job.

Soon enough, we have a magical trifecta: a plan, a parcel of land, and a contractor to start work!

Step #4: Develop

Armed with a great team, a great plan, and a piece of land purchased for a great price, it's time to start digging!

As soon as we start, of course, challenges pop up. There are always surprises—everything from thousands of buried tires to unexpected archaeological sites. That's normal, and although it can be stressful, we have contingencies in the budget. We know there will be hiccups, and we're prepared.

We start with water, sewer, roads, power, and other infrastructure. If you've ever driven past an open field with paved streets and pipes sticking out of the ground, you've seen a community in development.

Meanwhile, behind the scenes, the Development Services Team is doing all the paperwork. They track progress, updated plans when required, and communicate with the municipality. We also have to get a *plot* approved, which recognizes each new individual address at the municipal level. What started as "buy land, build a house" is a lot more complicated than it sounds!

Once the plot is recorded, our permitting department needs to apply for permits for each individual house. To do that, we need individual surveys and site plans for each lot. Those plans need to take into account setbacks and other restrictions. We'll also need structural engineering plans for the house itself and energy plans so we can calculate the HVAC requirements.

We bring all that to the municipality. Once the permits are approved, we can start building houses.

Step #5: Build

There is a magic moment when we actually pour the concrete slab for the foundation of a home. After months and months of preparation, we're *really* building a house.

Leading up to this moment, our Purchasing Team has been sourcing materials, assigning vendors, and issuing purchase orders. There might be 150 different POs on one home! Sometimes, those purchase orders aren't accepted, and we have to adjust or find new vendors.

If things go smoothly and there are no supply issues, we can build a house in 100 days in some areas. In other areas, it may take six to seven months.

Coordinating all the various vendors and trades and keeping everything on track is a big job. We have a full team of superintendents in the field whose job is to keep vendors on task and keep the project moving. At the same time, they also have the responsibility of keeping great relationships with them. Nothing helps us more than working with great teams through the entire process. The superintendents keep the projects moving but also keep our partners happy.

This is particularly tricky as we get into the finishing stages of a project. There are so many small details to finish a great home. As one person described it, "You're 90% done. You just have 50% more to do."

Eventually, however, we have a house. And that house is about to become a *home*.

Step #6: Rent

As the finishing touches and sign-offs happen, a new team arrives on the scene: our Leasing Department. Their job is to make sure the property is truly ready to be rented and to find a great tenant for the home.

During the final stages, we install an electronic deadbolt system that connects to our property management system. That allows us to pre-approve prospective tenants online, receive proof of identity, and send a lock code so they can see the house on their own.

It's a great way to give people the space they need to view a home with no pressure.

Much like a bank, our leasing department has criteria for tenants. No felonies or evictions. Certain earning requirements. We learned early on that proper screening takes time but actually speeds up the process and gets returns to our investors faster.

Finding the right tenant and keeping them happy is so important that we actually have as many people in leasing and management as we do in all of the other steps combined! Once we find a great tenant and they're approved, we sign a lease. The tenant makes a deposit, their move-in date is official, and the process is handed off to our Portfolio Management Team.

Step #7: Manage

If buying land is what ensures a good return, our Portfolio Management Team is what keeps that return low-effort and predictable for our investors. They're the people who make the whole process truly passive for our investors so that they can focus on their families.

The Portfolio Management Team deals with all the day-to-day operations until a tenant moves out, and we start the cycle all over again. From clogged drains to warranty claims, grass cutting to rent collection, they do it all.

Because we have a sister company on the build side, warranty issues are easy. Every new house needs a little attention, and we never have to worry about chasing down a vendor. Portfolio

Management takes care of all of it, keeps the tenants happy, and, because of that, keeps investors happy, too.

We learned the hard way that a property management team can be "stuck" between a tenant who needs something done, and a landlord who doesn't want to pay. It's a tough spot.

We've solved that by careful selection on both ends. In the beginning, we had to part ways with many landlords who didn't fit our standards. Now, we work with caring investors, and excellent long-term tenants. Better still, we're the builder! Quality construction and reliable warranty service are built right in.

That vertical integration is crucial for you, the investor. The *only* way to know your investment isn't going to become a second job is to have exceptional property management. That's even *more* critical when you go out of state, or international.

We're in over a dozen markets now in Florida alone. Before we build in a market, we always set up portfolio management first. I learned the hard way that you can buy a house for 50 cents on the dollar, but if you have no management in place, you can still lose money.

We have continued to uplevel our property management process and guidelines over the years. We've really staffed up this team. If there's a problem, we have someone for it! For every market we build in, we have management set up before we even start. It's one of the areas I'm most proud of, and it's a huge reason our tenants and investors stay for the long term.

The Investor Journey

The road to development can be winding, but we eventually get there. We reach our goal of creating a great home for a great family so we can start delivering great returns to investors.

I know many individual investors who have the experience and skills to do a single BTR project. They have a construction or development background and have the capital and experience to see a project through. They follow the same steps as we do for a large project, but most of the steps are far less complex, happen faster, and require less overhead.

That can seem appealing—and for the right person, it is. But there are some downsides.

•**Time.** Because we're working at scale, we always have a home that's ready to rent, or close to ready, for an investor to invest in. Building on your own can mean waiting a year—frequently more—to finally move in a tenant and start the "rent" part of BTR investing.

•**Capital.** Time, of course, is also money. That long stretch of development is a time of lots of money out, with no money in. You need the financial runway to see the project through. We're able to shorten the timeline because we're building at scale. In addition, as interest rates have increased, we've created in-house financing options for our investors that can be 2-3% below traditional mortgage company rates.

•**Return.** Even for people with the skills, building a single, brand-new home for rent is hard. We build at scale. We buy windows by the thousands. Doors by the hundreds. Wood by the ton. That gives us a significant advantage on the cost side so we can deliver better returns.

•**Passivity.** Even new properties need management, and this is another area where larger BTR companies shine. Our management is top-notch and ensures that investors get passive income, not a second job.

The lesson? Unless you have the relevant experience and abundant capital, most investors are better off finding an excellent BTR partner with a proven track record.

The BTR Difference

Recently, I got a message from an investor that his insurance on a property had skyrocketed at renewal. Within a few minutes our team had connected him with one of our preferred vendors. That same day, he had a quote that saved him $5,000.

That's the value of having an experienced team with an extensive network.

Yes, there are other ways to passively invest in real estate. Funds, syndication, REITs, fractional ownership—they all provide exposure to the same industry. Many are great ways to accomplish the same goal.

In our experience, they're simply not *as* great for two reasons:

1.**Ownership.** Direct property ownership is one of the most proven ways for long-term wealth creation in real estate. Many of the approaches above offer shared, little, or no direct ownership.

2.Quality. Most of the time, when you hear about "turn-key real estate," you're hearing about old properties. Those properties have challenges. We focus on new builds with warranties because we know quality leads to true passive income. We're a dedicated team, with a dedicated purpose.

Is it all worth it? If you're still wondering, let's compare three options.

Five years ago, if you invested $250,000 in:

• **The S&P 500**, your average return would be 10.495% earning you $131,187.50 over 5 years
• **A performing real estate fund**, your average return would be 13.5% earning you $168,750 over 5 years

However, if you had taken that same $250, 000 and invested it in a **Southern Impression Homes new construction rental property** in Jacksonville, Florida, **your average return would be 264.20% earning you $660,500.**

(Based on 5 Single-Family Rentals with equity growth & 10% cash flow growth annually.)

Those numbers aren't even close. Once gain, it's real estate for the win.

It's been a long road to reach a place where we're fully vertically integrated and can handle all the moving parts of a great BTR investment. We can find the land, we can develop it, we can manage the property, and we can finance it for investors. If it sounds passive for our investors, it's because it is.

Chapter 6 Key Points

•There are seven stages in a BTR project—whether it's a single infill lot or an entire community: acquire, evaluate, purchase, develop, build, rent, and manage.

•Each step is carefully designed to accomplish the end goal of a great family in a great home, providing great passive returns to investors.

•Compared to "DIY" BTR, an established firm offers time, capital, return, and passivity advantages.

•Unlike syndication, REITs, BTR has the advantage of direct ownership and high-quality new construction.

CHAPTER SEVEN
Build to Live

From BTR to a Legendary Family

"I always had a knack for planning ahead," David Phelps wrote. "I had laid out my entire life in advance. Failure was not an option." An aspiring dentist, David was determined to have it all—a perfect career, a perfect family, a perfect life.

As a senior in college, he took an interest in wealth-building, reading books about the stock market and real estate investing. Real estate won hands down, and in his first year of college, David convinced his father to partner on a two-story brick rental in Dallas. It was the worst house in a good neighborhood.

Meanwhile, David waited tables through college and planned his dentistry future. When he and his father sold the property and split the gains, David realized he'd made ten times more from that one transaction than he had in all his long nights and weekends waiting tables.

The lightbulb came on. "Why should I work for money all of my life," he asked, "when I could acquire good capital assets that would work for me whether I worked or not?"

That became the plan: While David built his practice, he would continue to invest in real estate. And for nearly twenty years, that's exactly what he did. Good real estate. Acquired carefully. Financed correctly. Managed properly.

Planning ahead. David's specialty.

The Epiphany

But not everything can be planned.

That became apparent when David's daughter, Jenna, faced a series of health crises. High-risk leukemia at age two. Seizures from age eight to twelve. And now, while David sat on a bench in a hospital room, Jenna lay beside him, recovering from six hours of challenging transplant surgery to replace her failed liver and save her life. As he later wrote:

"Disconnected from the rest of the world, nothing else mattered. All of the daily "stuff" that had seemed so paramount wasn't even a blip on my radar.

All of my education, wisdom, and experience; even all of the money I could earn – none of it mattered. None of it could make a difference.

I could only hope.

Hope and pray that Jenna would recover and I would get a second chance. A second chance to be a father – a real father who would be present, not absent. Not preoccupied with "stuff."

Would there be a "someday?" A day in the future when I could spend quality time with Jenna?"[3]

"I loved what I did," David said, "but the epiphany was that there was more to my life. I was giving up all this time to build some imaginary fortress—financial security for my family. But I couldn't do anything about my daughter's health situation. All the money in the world, all the real estate, wasn't going to buy her back if something happened."

"I had come to the realization," he said, "that I was putting off that time to some distant future that might never come."

The Big Lie

As entrepreneurs and successful professionals, we tell ourselves a story. It's a story about how we're *providing*. How we're growing a business for our family. Building wealth for our family. Working long hours for our family.

But at a certain level of abundance and accomplishment, the "I'm providing" story no longer holds up.

This is what I call the Big Lie of Entrepreneurship. It's a lie that tells us that one day, it will all be different. One day, if we get the business to X or our investments to Y, then everything will be perfect. *Then*, and only then, we'll have time to focus on things like our health and our hearts.

Of course, that day never comes. And over time, the Big Lie steals from us. The business takes us from our family. Our work slowly chips away at the limited time we have on the planet with the people who matter most.

The Big Lie works by giving us *permission*. It gives us the latitude to put finances before family. To put business before relationships, work before kids.

But there are moments when the lie is revealed. Times when we see past it and we realize that time is running out. In the hospital at his daughter's bedside, David had his moment. And in it, he made a choice: he would leave private practice. David was done with dentistry.

Fresh Permission

Real estate gave David the opportunity to leave his work and focus on his family. It was the Plan B that became Plan A. Passive income meant he could do what many families could not.

But for David, it wasn't just a question of math. He recalls that time in the hospital as *giving him permission to look at life differently.* He had spent almost two decades telling himself, "I'm a doctor. I have to grind. I have to be there. Everybody needs me. If I'm not there, I'm not making any money."

Sitting beside his daughter, David began to question those assumptions.

"I had to sit in the hospital and go, 'Okay, David, how much is enough? How much is enough for me to actually take the time that I want so badly right now to invest in my daughter and not have to feel guilty about it?'"

Passive income gave financial freedom to David, but it was his daughter Jenna who gave him the *emotional* freedom to put it to use.

Like David, you may need to grant yourself permission, too. To decide *I no longer have permission to put my family second*. To know that what you do have is the permission to put your precious time where it matters most.

Real estate may be history's greatest wealth-building tool. But it's still a tool. It's a means to a legendary family life, but it's not the end. As David says, "Real estate is just the vehicle."

Where you drive it is up to you.

Build to Live

David did leave private practice. And he would go on to start a business that helps dentists like him use the power of passive income to create family freedom.

Jenna, however, still had a difficult road ahead. She had already undergone intense chemotherapy for leukemia. She had suffered through the epileptic seizures for four years. Now, the liver transplant left her facing yet another long recovery.

It had taken a toll. At the age of sixteen, Jenna was still reading and writing at a second-grade level. But she was, and is, a fighter. She would go on to rise above the challenges to become a college graduate, a published author, and a speaker.

And David? He's found perspective.

"People think there's some mountain peak they have to hit," he said. "But every time you hit a mountain peak, there's a next one to hit. There's another. Oh, there's another."

His real estate portfolio now includes build-to-rent—a decision that aligns with his perspective.

"Build-To-Rent is a model that has so many built-in safety nets for more sustainable, predictable income," he said. "You've got warranties. It attracts the right tenants. You have less turnover and lower maintenance costs. You're not going to have any major mechanical, roof, structure, foundations, plumbing, sewer, or electrical problems.

"I want sustainable, predictable," he said. "I don't want the ups and downs, ups and downs. And that's what that build-to-rent model gives." In a life filled with ups and downs, David, perhaps, knows the value of a stable income better than anyone.

You could call Jenna lucky. David and his wife, too. They not only faced an extraordinarily difficult set of challenges but were given the wake-up call that set them on course for their legendary family life.

I think David would say that luck isn't a plan. And he would never wish upon anyone the circumstances that led to his epiphany. But you don't *have* to face a life-or-death situation to commit to change. You do, however, have to *decide*: What comes first—your family or your business?

Our Legendary Family is Born

As I wound my way through the challenges of growing a business, I repeatedly saw the power of real estate to change lives for the better. But I often saw things I didn't like, too.

I saw people who were successful by every financial measure but whose relationships were a disaster or whose health was failing. These were people I admired, and their lives were in shambles.

When I met Jamie, something changed in me. She was divorced with full custody of two beautiful little boys. Suddenly, there were a little seven-year-old and a five-year-old looking for a father figure. I was running two real estate businesses and just coming out of near-extinction. All I could think was *I don't want to mess this up.*

When we added two more children to our family, that feeling only escalated. As our family grew, my father's story felt relevant in a way it never had before. I wanted to be there for them. Like David and so many others, I knew I had a decision to make. Was I going to be there for them, or was I going to let work and business take all of me?

One year at Christmas, I took the most tangible step I could think of to make what I felt *real*: I gave the boys quality time coupons. There was one for every 90 days. We called them "Jim Day" coupons. I told the boys they could cash in a coupon, and the day would be theirs. I'd do anything they wanted. My phone would be off. They would get my complete attention.

The kids were used to me having appointments for work, so I used that language to make it feel as important as I could. "It's our big meeting," I told them. "An important board meeting."

That was the genesis moment. As our family grew from two to five kids, our Family Board Meeting practice would become the keystone rhythm of our family. We would go on to improve it with each year, striving to make it more meaningful and using it to create deeper, lasting connections with our kids.

And then we would bring it to the wider world.

—ele—

You can think of this book as asking and answering two questions.

The first is *how can I create true passive income using real estate?*

The answer, we believe, lies in the power of build-to-rent.

The second question is, *how do I use that to create a legendary family life?*

In Part III, we're going to answer that question by showing you the exact strategies and tools that we use—including the Family Board Meeting that started it all. They are the same ones we've passed on to thousands of families. They're tried, they're tested, and they *work*.

All the money in the world won't create a legendary family. It won't let you live forever, and it won't turn back the clock.

But you can use the abundance around you to *change the rhythm of your life*. And in doing so, you can create connections that last.

Here's how.

Chapter 7 Key Points

•The Big Lie of entrepreneurship gives us permission to overwork and to put off our most important relationships to "someday."

•Real estate may be the greatest wealth-building tool in history, but it's only a tool. You get to choose how to use it.

•Passive income can provide financial freedom. It's up to you to give yourself the emotional freedom to use it wisely.

•What comes first—your family or your business?

PART 3
Build To Live

CHAPTER EIGHT

The Legendary Family Elements

T he Ingredients for Lasting Bonds

Years ago, I went to an addiction treatment center to help a friend going through detox. On the last day of the program, most people brought a family member with them for support. Those family members were, more often than not, parents.

As the day progressed, I realized those parents had something in common. Beyond the painful challenge of a child struggling with addiction, *they were all very successful.*

Every parent in the room was an accomplished entrepreneur or established professional. They had all found financial success. But they had also paid a price. They'd sacrificed quality time for wealth, and their families had suffered horribly.

As I wrote in *The Family Board Meeting*:

"That day, I watched successful grown men and women sobbing at the clear knowledge they hadn't been there for their children when it was most important. It was enough to change me forever. That day, I learned there was something more important than money,

more important than fancy private schools and more important than empty gifts. That's something that's called quality time.

I sat in that room listening to the devastating stories and the heart-wrenching regret of each parent as a hundred different threads wound themselves together in my mind. The disconnected entrepreneurs and corporate warriors I'd met over the years, the disconnected parents in the support group, the memory of my friend's disconnected upbringing. It was like a slap in the face, an abrupt shock that left me wondering, what happened to these families?"

Like many entrepreneurs, I drew strength from my ability to work hard. I knew I had hustle. I knew I could grind. I could put my head down and make things happen. By the time I met Jamie and adopted my two older sons, I was running two businesses and putting those strengths to work.

But in the back of my mind, a voice kept reminding me of those families in pain. All of them successful, all of them running businesses. All of them running. That was when I began to realize my strengths could also be my downfall.

Forbes Magazine[4] found that America's richest billionaires get divorced around 49% of the time. The surprise? That statistic is roughly the same as it is for *all* marriages.

Having boatloads of money doesn't create happiness. It doesn't shelter you from hard times, challenging emotions, or family crises. Grind, hustle, and wealth won't make your family stronger.

This chapter will tell you what does. In it, we'll show you exactly how your BTR passive income can fuel the strong bonds that build legendary families.

The Four Elements

Success can create legendary families, or it can destroy them. That's the truth I witnessed at the treatment center, and it was a difficult pill to swallow.

Over the years, I've come to understand a deeper truth: *it's easier to be a good entrepreneur than a parent*. It's easier to work hard professionally than it is to truly show up as a mom or a dad.

But you *need* to show up. You need to build a business around your life, not the other way around. As Jamie says, scaling our business will never come before the foundation of our marriage, our family, or our friendships.

Still, as any dedicated professional will tell you, that's much easier to say than to *do*.

What follows is a set of principles that drive deep family connection. If you're wearing your business hat, think of them as a strategic plan for your most important relationships. We call these principles the four elements of a legendary family: *time*, *adventure*, *connection*, and *value*.

Element #1: Time

A friend of mine owned a large healthcare practice, and he was going through a rough patch. Business had gone poorly. He'd been through a contentious divorce. His ego had taken a beating, and he had two twin girls who he wanted to stay connected to more than anything.

He was in one of our mastermind groups and made a decision to embrace Family Board Meetings as a way to foster that connection—a strategy you'll learn more about in the next chapter.

My friend committed to an undistracted day, one-on-one, with each of his twin daughters. When I checked in with him, he described how each daughter, independently, had told him the same thing: "Dad, we don't care about the business. We just want you."

"That moment," he said, "was an absolute *a-ha*. It changed me."

Knowing that his value as a father wasn't about his professional success became a source of comfort. It gave him new confidence. It shifted the way he saw his work and changed how he rebuilt his business. Like David in the previous chapter, it gave him permission to think differently about his life.

Here's the takeaway: that *a-ha* moment was only made possible by *time*.

Not just any time. *Quality* time. Dedicated one-on-one time with his children that offered the space and emotional room for deep connection.

If the term feels vague, that's fair. Let's pin it down. Quality time is *not* driving around with your kid in the back seat while you take calls. Quality time isn't being home but spending all day in your home office.

Quality time is *intentional*. It's planned. It's strategic. You prepare for quality time like it's as important as a key business meeting.

Because it is.

Of the four, time is the "master element." Without it, it's very difficult to share adventures, create solid connections, or teach values.

How do you know if you're giving quality time to your kids? You answer a single question—the question we consider "the most important question in the world."

When was the last time you spent a half-day or more, one-on-one with your child, with no electronics?

If your answer is "I don't know," then the next question you'll want to ask yourself is *why?*

Element #2: Adventure

You could substitute the word *fun* here. After all, that's what we're driving at. If you give time to your family, but that time isn't enjoyable, then no one will want more of it.

We prefer the word *adventure*. When we hear it, we think of excitement and exploration and being in the moment. If you say, "Let's have an adventure," we can think of ten ideas. If you say, "Let's have fun," it feels a little vague.

Adventure doesn't have to be a week on a tropical island. Adventures are everywhere, from your backyard to the local park. Adventures can be free, and they can be effortless. Most of all, they can be *fun*.

Adventure is a way of taking the *time* you're creating for your family (element #1) and making it enjoyable. That means you'll keep doing it!

But there's more here.

Emotions change us. Our memories of emotional events are often more vivid, accurate, and easier to remember.[5] If you can recall in great detail your first kiss or your wedding day or the day your child was born, you've experienced this. Those moments were infused with emotion, so they stay with you.

That is what you're trying to do with time—to add emotional power to the things you do so that they become more memorable. Because when your moments as a family become more memorable, you get our next element....

Element #3: Connection

When you take the first element of time and multiply it by the power of adventure, something magical begins to happen: you *connect*. You might think of it as a legendary family formula:

Time x Adventure=Connection

For much of human history, being connected to others meant survival. Social connection is deeply wired into our evolution.

That legacy is still with us. Research has shown that a lack of social connection is worse for your health than obesity, smoking, and high blood pressure![6]

When we share emotional moments, we connect. When we connect, we become healthier and happier. A connected family is bonded by trust, respect, and loyalty. That lays the groundwork for what might be the most important job in modern families: teaching and sharing values.

Element #4: Values

There seem to be endless stories of lottery players who win millions and lose it all. (And then some.[7]) Passive income, it turns out, needs *guardrails*. If you hit the jackpot, it doesn't mean anything if that jackpot pushes you off a cliff.

In the case of a legendary family life, these guardrails are *values*. They act as a filter through which you make decisions. They are the core principles that determine how you see the world, choose what is most important, and take action. When people say *money makes you more of what you already are*, that's what they mean: money magnifies your *true* values.

We did a core values exercise with our kids where we were encouraged as a family to come up with the things that matter most to us and then to draw them.

In the end, we came up with a drawing of a huge surfboard surrounded by stick figures for all of our family members, each surfing a wave. (And one mermaid, Jamie.)

Written on the surfboard were the family values we'd listed as most important:

- Love
- Loyalty
- Creativity
- Abundance
- Service
- Humor

- Health
- Sobriety
- Adventure
- Faith
- Freedom

I sometimes refer to these values as a spaghetti strainer. They're the filter that we pass our decisions through, big or small. What sticks to the values stays in our lives. The rest we let go.

We have always led with our family values. Others used to think it was a little unorthodox or wonky. But it has made all the difference.

Now, we're privileged to help other families lead in the same way. When we get a message like, "Thanks to you, I'm on a boat with my teenagers this week having a remarkable family vacation," I think *that's values at work.*

Elemental Flow

The four elements of a legendary family life don't operate in a vacuum. There's a natural flow.

- *Time.* The great enabler. Without time, all relationships eventually fray. To make time enjoyable, we add...
- *Adventure.* It makes the time fun, so you want to do more of it, and adds the emotional juice that allows for...

•*Connection.* What we truly crave. A truly close and happy family lets us share...

•*Values.* The core beliefs and principles on which we raise children and build strong families and communities.

Each element serves the next. Together, they build the base for legendary families.

The Money Talk: Managing the Impact of Money on Legendary Families

Even with good intentions and all four elements, prosperous families face a challenge that many don't. It's a good problem to have, but it's a problem nonetheless: how to manage the impact of wealth.

That day at the addiction treatment center was a cautionary tale for me. Every person in that room was the child of an entrepreneur or a successful professional. But they were also exposed to money at a young age. I began to wonder—could money itself be a problem?

I decided that if we were going to have money, we needed to also give our kids the tools they needed to manage it in a healthy way.

At the age of 16, our son Alden approached us with a goal. He wanted to be a millionaire before the age of 30.

We never pushed Alden—or any of our kids—to follow us. We tried to provide lessons in financial intelligence along the way, and we watched his drive and initiative grow as he experimented.

Now, he wanted more. It was time for a talk.

We've all heard of the "sex talk," but most of us shy from what might be a far more critical conversation—what I call the "money talk."

My friend Don Wenner knows his share about these conversations. His investment company has entrusted over $40 million into housing projects with us, and has been ranked on the Inc. 5000 list of "Fastest Growing Private Companies in America" for ten consecutive years. Don's a dedicated husband and father of three boys. He described to me once why these conversations matter so much:

"People think it's bad investment decisions, or they didn't have the appropriate estate planning. It's rarely those reasons. It's a parenting crisis, not a financial planning crisis.

The first generation wealth creators—the business owners, entrepreneurs, executives—that wealth typically is lost, if not by their children, then their grandchildren."

The money talk is a critical step in avoiding this generational crisis. Don't shy away from it.

Our money talk began with a disclaimer Alden had heard many times: We support your talents and drive, and we want to provide opportunities we didn't have. But we won't do the work for you, and we won't hand you anything.

I reminded him that our family finances are tied to our core values. Choosing a path that strays from these values, such as addiction, means we can't provide those opportunities.

My son knows me well, and he knew there was no wiggle room in that statement. I won't budge. I love him too much to even consider it.

Our Money Talk took place in the mastermind room at my office. On a whiteboard, I outlined our different businesses, real estate, and other assets. I explained how each worked and how they make money (or sometimes lose it). I told him the pros and the cons. It was a simple but complete look at our financial life.

I explained to Alden how, as a young man, I had the same goal he did. And that I did indeed become a millionaire by age 28. Then a multi-millionaire by 30.

I could tell that excited him. But like sex talks, money talks aren't just about the fun parts. I told Alden how, after just two years, I almost lost everything. At 32, I was a negative millionaire and had to start again. I shared with him what I did right, and what I did wrong, and where it had led us to in the present.

On a second whiteboard, we connected his goals with a simple plan that would let him accomplish his dreams while still enjoying his life. This was entirely based on a path he chose. His dreams were about his interests, not mine.

Since Alden left traditional school almost five years earlier, I had always encouraged him to be on the lookout for three things:

- What do you enjoy?
- What are naturally good at?
- What does the world need?

It was a simple formula taught to me by a mentor when I was in my 30s, and one I wished I'd known at Alden's age.

Where those questions intersect for Alden is in the ocean.

His goal was to have his own charter fishing businesses. He loves being on the water, and fishing lights him up. He has a natural gift for it. And in beautiful areas like the Florida Keys, the world is in great need of these services and pays well for them.

In our money talk, I showed him how he could invest the earnings from doing what he loves into a simple retirement plan, side hustle business, and investment properties. I told him how we could help, but also reminded him that the heavy lifting was his. It was his business to build, and his goal to reach.

We both left the meeting with a smile, a feeling of excitement and a greater respect for one another. He must have said thank you a half-dozen times, and was filled with my own gratitude for being able to have a money talk with my kids that my parents were never able to have with me.

Wealth is just a tool. Many wealthy people don't establish values in their family. They don't think about what they want their wealth to do or to the traps they want to avoid.

That's a recipe for disappointment and destruction. Don't skip the sex talk. But make sure you add the money talk to your family!

Is It a REAL Priority?

You can sum up all four elements in one idea: A legendary life is about *putting your family first*.

In over a dozen years of helping thousands of families build legendary lives, I've found that the people who are able to put family first are almost always happier. They thrive.

Conversely, when you build your life so that your family gets what is left over *after* work? Well, there's usually not much left.

Everyone says, "My family is my top priority." What else would you say? But talk is cheap. You have to do more than tell your family they're your priority. You have to *show* them. And that's where things get tricky.

Showing is hard because showing *up* is hard. Life can be unpredictable. If you have found yourself struggling to make family a priority, *you are not alone*. We've all been there. We've all felt the tug of war between the desires of our personal lives and the demands of our work. It's not easy.

But we can help make it easier.

In the next chapter, we're going to give you a toolbox for *actually* putting your family first. Four family rhythms that will add more time, connection, adventure, and values to your legendary life.

Chapter 8 Key Points

•Wealth doesn't shelter your family from difficulties, challenging emotions, or family crises.

•Success can help create legendary families, or it can destroy them.

•There are four elements to a legendary family: *time*, *adventure*, *connection*, and *value*.

•A legendary life is about putting your family first.

CHAPTER NINE

The 4 Rhythms

How Legendary Families Come Alive

One busy day, I came home from work to find my daughter Maggie brimming with energy. She was five and at a beautiful age when she loved to play with her dad. I was happy to oblige.

"Daddy, let's go on the trampoline," she said, practically bouncing off the tile floor.

A few minutes later, we were jumping and laughing together. I was completely in the moment. It was like I was five, too—carefree and soaking up a beautiful sunny day.

And then I heard a sound.

Suddenly, I wasn't five anymore. I was a grown-up. I wasn't jumping on the trampoline. I was standing still, distracted. It was like the sound had flipped a switch in my brain.

The sound was my phone. I'd accidentally left it in my pocket. I knew better, but in the chaos of the day's end, I'd forgotten. And now it was calling to me.

I tried to ignore it, but the damage was done. The message could have been about any one of the ten different challenges that day, but once the spell was broken, it didn't matter which one it was. I couldn't seem to let it go.

And so I took my phone out. The message was about a small detail on a property closing—a simple title issue I had dealt with hundreds of times. In the big scheme of things, it was meaningless.

But it had interrupted the moment. The spell was broken, and the damage was done.

The Four Rhythms

You can have passive income and still be a ghost in your family.

That was the *a-ha* moment for me on the trampoline. For all our success, knowledge, and years helping families connect, it only took one phone call to derail a perfect moment with my daughter.

I *know* that quality family time matters. We literally wrote the book on it. I *know* that time, connection, adventure, and values create legendary families.

But that doesn't mean that prioritizing these elements is *easy*.

To make your family a priority, you need to do more than just talk about it. You need strategies that keep your family resilient in the face of the uncertainties of everyday life. Life is going to keep being demanding—you need tools to deal with it. You need to find ways to ensure that you don't succeed at work, but fail at home.

Enter the four rhythms.

Over the years, we've developed a tool kit for reinforcing the four legendary family elements. The tool kit is an easy-to-follow set of practices that make it easier to put family first. They're fun. They're simple. And best of all, *they work*. They make sure that magical moments with your children happen and remain unspoiled.

We know from helping thousands of families that *legendary families are a discipline.* The elements of the previous chapter are the blueprint for the family we want to build, but *the rhythms are the toolkit for actually doing it.* They are:

1. Family Board Meetings
2. Date Night with a Question
3. Family Masterminds
4. Sunday Dinner

Rhythm# 1: Family Board Meetings

When we first began to develop our blueprint for quality time, we didn't know what to call our approach.

I love surfing. When surfers talk about having a "board meeting," they're not in the boardroom. They're out on their surfboards. Our family always prioritized time on the beach, and we began to call our quality time a *family board meeting*, mixing the idea of an important business meeting with the fun of being out on our boards.

The name stuck. Over time, we took the idea and built more structure around it. It's very simple, and anyone can implement it.

There are just three rules:

•**One-on-one.** In a legendary family life, you strengthen the whole by separating and investing in the parts. Once per quarter, plan at least a half day of *one-on-one* time with each child, doing an activity that *they* chose.

•**No electronics.** Simple, yes. But don't fool yourself. Like me, it's easy to forget to turn your phone off or to "sneak a peek" at your messages and ruin a perfect moment. Don't do it.

•**Focused reflection.** To solidify the experience into real connection, ask a gentle, intentional question before the day ends, like, "What was your favorite part of today?"

That's it. It's deceptively simple, but the combination of the three is what I call an "unfair advantage" for creating a deeper and more meaningful connection with your children.

You can learn more about family board meetings in our book or by visiting 18summers.com/ .

Rhythm #2: Date Night with a Question

The single greatest threat to your financial abundance and passive income isn't the economy. It's not your income. It's *divorce*. Breaking up a committed relationship can instantly cut each partner's net worth in half while doubling their cost of living. And that's just the math. The emotional toll is much higher and touches every part of your life.

Like every family, Jamie and I faced our share of challenges as we grew our life and business. As we wrote about it in the most recent edition of *The Family Board Meeting:*

The next few years would challenge us. We were in the process of growing our family from two kids to five, and that journey wasn't easy. There were miscarriages, disappointments, and a lot of heartache. Along the way, the 2008 real estate meltdown would threaten everything we'd built.

It was serious. It was hard. But we were determined to not let the world break us.

By then, we already had Family Board Meetings in place, and they had been so effective in connecting us with our kids. We thought, *why not use this in our relationship?*

Jamie and I decided we would have a regular date night—like a Family Board Meeting, but every week. It took a few embarrassing failed attempts to figure out how to make a date night *really* work, but we eventually created a rhythm that works every time.

Like a board meeting, Date Night with a Question follows a similar three-part strategy:

1. Set the rhythm. Date night *must* go on the calendar, preferably at the same time and day each week. Ours is every Wednesday.

2. Ditch the distractions. Silence those devices. Keep them out of sight. If you need to be reached, use the do not disturb feature on your phone.

3. Bring a question. We bring a question to date night and take turns presenting it to each other—things like, "Who was your most influential teacher?" or "Can you tell me a time when you felt most close to me?"

Your relationship might be new. It might be decades old. But no matter how long you've been together, remember: never stop dating your spouse!

Note: you can find a big list of free date night questions at 18Summers.com/Bonus-Downloads.

Rhythm #3: Family Masterminds

Board meetings and date nights are rhythms that draw their value from consistency. We repeat them regularly because we know that over time, they connect us.

Family masterminds are different. They're based on problem-solving. Rather than being dictated by a schedule, they're an "on-demand" family meeting to solve a problem or make decisions as a group. We've used them to do everything from planning family vacations to dealing with difficult health issues.

When someone in our family needs support or input, we rally as a team. We sit around a table, and we talk it out. We might pull out a whiteboard, or we might call another friend in our network for help. The kids bring their friends, too. We've covered everything from money to education to relationships to business, but the philosophy is always the same: *we're a team, and this is how we help each other.*

Family masterminds have no hard rules. But they do have three principles that help make them effective:

•**Safe space.** Any topic is welcome. No problem is too small. Open discussion is key, and it only works if the kids feel like they can tell the truth. Nothing shuts a kid down faster than being criticized for sharing their struggles. Masterminds aren't for judging. They're for listening, supporting, and taking action when necessary.

•**Accountability.** Simply listening without judgment goes a long way. But families need to take action, too. Holding people accountable is a powerful tool, and it goes both ways. We hold the kids accountable in masterminds, and they hold us accountable, too.

•**Fun.** No one needs more boring meetings in their life, especially kids. We've used masterminds to play games like Cashflow. It's a fun way to teach principles of wealth. We've also read books as a family and then come together to talk about them. Masterminds aren't just about gathering for damage control. They're about joining up to support each other and grow together.

Worried? Call a family mastermind. Planning a trip? Call a mastermind. Feeling disconnected? Yep—mastermind. Unlike the other scheduled rhythms, a mastermind can be called at any time. It's a critical on-the-fly tool for any legendary family.

Rhythm #4: Sunday Dinner

I read that sixty years ago, the average dinner time was just over ninety minutes. Now, it's in the neighborhood of twelve.

When I read that, I couldn't get it out of my mind. So much lost family time! For me, mealtimes represent a unique opportunity for families to connect while enjoying something everyone loves: great food.

When I really got honest, however, I realized a lot of our mealtimes were being lost to the chaos of a busy week. Around the same time, the boys had begun to make comments about how they never really knew when I was traveling for work. It bothered them to have me come and go, seemingly at random.

It hit me: these two problems were one opportunity.

I began to wonder how we could solve our family logistics challenge and, at the same time, turn meals into something more significant—something closer to what they might have been when my parents were kids.

The starting point for that was Sunday dinner. There wasn't anything particularly magical about Sunday—except for us, there was. Like most families, Sunday was the one night of the week we were most likely to all be together with the time to connect. The rest of the week might be a hurricane of work and sports and appointments and commitments, but Sundays seemed to offer a window of relative calm in the storm.

We began to use Sunday dinners to draw out the meal a little longer and leverage the opportunity we had together. Our Sunday meals (for us, it's as many in a week as we can, but we start with Sundays) work best by keeping three things in mind:

•**No tech.** We have a no electronics policy not just at the dinner table but for the time leading up to *and* following the meal. That not only keeps us in the moment while we eat, but it also allows the kids to more easily help with dinner prep and clean up.

•**Best & weirdest.** This is the family version of an icebreaker. We go around the table, and everyone says the best thing and the strangest thing that happened to them that day/week. It sounds simple, but it leads to lots of laughs and gratitude—and *everyone* gets to participate.

•**Logistics.** Finally, the Sunday meeting gets everyone in the same place to discuss plans for the following week. Who needs to be where and when? Who's working? Who needs help studying for a test? Who's got a doctor's appointment or a baseball game? In a family with five kids, logistics matter. But they also mean more than scheduling. Figuring out the week gets kids talking, and it also shows them how much they matter.

Don't let this overwhelm you. The habit of the meal matters far more than the number per week. You don't need to do Sunday, and you don't need to do it every day. Aim for one day a week to start. If you can do more, that's great. But take consistency over quantity.

The Rhythm Makes the Music

Nothing happens in the dark in our family.

I started our real estate journey alone, but it became clear early on that I could no longer be an island. This wasn't *my* real estate business—it was *ours*. It wasn't *my* passive income or *my* legendary family—these things were ours to build and share.

That shift defines our family. We aren't just relating together, we're *creating* together.

Jamie began attending accounting meetings because she was just as valuable a stakeholder as I was. We had seen too many relationships where each partner was a silo. That was a recipe for eventual misunderstanding, resentment, and, for some families, deception. Those things are anything but legendary.

Jamie now has a huge role in managing not just our family but the vacation rental side of our business, our workshops, books, and more. She's part of the entire picture at a high level.

The same applies to our kids. They come to meetings, too. When we were working to write this book, the kids sat down to be interviewed. They had input on everything from the title and cover to the deepest themes. They are as wired into the fabric of this book as they are into our family life.

As with music, rhythm is what we feel most deeply. It's what moves us most. The four rhythms don't just create time together. They *integrate* your family. They connect threads between all the people and parts of your life. They bring out the best and help avoid the worst. They are the discipline that turns a group of individual personalities, hopes, and dreams into a *family*.

Chapter 9 Key Points

•You can have passive income and still be a ghost in your family.

•To build connections and reinforce the core elements of legendary families, you need simple practices that are easy to follow, enjoyable, and repeatable.

•The four rhythms are *Family Board Meetings, Date Night with a Question, Family Masterminds,* and *Sunday Dinner*

•Legendary families don't just relate—they *create*.

CHAPTER TEN

The Passive Income Playbook

The Hidden Upsides of BTR

You might say real estate is in Tom Tousignant's blood.

His grandfather started a real estate company that survived the Great Depression and World War II. Both Tom's father and five of his uncles followed a similar path.

When Tom left the Air Force and was later laid off from his commercial airline position, he turned to real estate, too—in his case, the mortgage business.

Like his family before him, real estate served him well. By the age of 58, Tom was ready to retire. For Tom, however, traditional investing—things like stocks and bonds, for example—created emotional complications in retirement.

"You go to a traditional financial planner," he said, "and they're all about building up this bucket of money. And you're going to draw down this bucket. Drawing down a bucket of money is pretty depressing."

Tom was touching on one of the great unspoken advantages of real estate for older investors: it provides cash flow without "drawing down the bucket." (In fact, the bucket grows.)

"People can't figure out how to turn a 401K into cashflow," Tom said, "and so they think, 'I don't know if I have enough money, so I'm going to work for one more year.'"

That year becomes a second year. Then, a third year. And so on.

BTR and Uncertainty Management

The trap is uncertainty. Retirees worry about markets, lifespan, and healthcare costs—and they have no way to predict any of it.

BTR changes this emotional trap in three meaningful ways:

1. Stable Cash Flow

Even with a generous allowance for maintenance, Tom knows exactly what will be left at the end of every month. This is particularly true with his BTR investments.

Like many older properties, Tom's cash flowed well for a short period. Now, it's routine for him to have a surprise two- or three-thousand-dollar expense every other month, making the income less reliable.

Compare that to one of his BTR properties. At the five-year mark, there was a tenant changeover. The only cost was to wash the floors and touch up the paint. It cost $800.

Tom's real estate creates reliable passive income without the fear of slowly shrinking his asset base.

2. Equity Growth

With income real estate, you're not forced to draw down the bucket. You're not forced to sell assets. In fact—your assets *grow*.

Tom's existing older homes have all gone up some 50% in five or six years. His BTR investments have done even better. "My new homes have pretty much all doubled in value," he said.

BTR offers a steady stream of golden eggs without pressure to eat the goose itself.

3. Tax Advantages

The traditional retirement model focuses on deferring taxes to a time when you can live on less. At that point, you slowly sell your assets (draw down the bucket) and pay less tax on income because your income is lower.

Not everyone, however, wants to live a smaller life in retirement. Add to that the uncertainties of markets and health and lifespan, and many people keep working when they'd like to retire and spend more time with family. Similarly, not everyone wants to be forced to sell their assets, which tax-deferred accounts require.

Income real estate offers a unique approach: simply refinance properties, take that money tax-free, and have someone else (the tenants) pay it back.

All told, these build-to-rent advantages grant older investors a unique gift: peace of mind.

"I'm really grateful that what we have is going to be enough," Tom said. "It's given me more time to make better decisions. I'm much better positioned for whatever happens. When I was working sixty hours a week in the mortgage business, I didn't have time to think about that."

Now, Tom's passive income supports a passion he's had since he was young. He spends much of his free time with airplanes—flying them or looking at buying and selling them. More important, it's connected him to his own legendary family life. "Just this year," he said, "I hiked in Wyoming with my son in the Grand Tetons. I went skydiving with my daughter in San Diego. I went skiing in Colorado with my other son. I get to travel with my wife."

Tom's 60th birthday is approaching. Recently, he found a picture taken at the beach on his forty-first birthday. He showed it to his wife. She said, "You look a lot better now."

"There's a noticeable difference," Tom agreed. "I was getting a lot more aches and pains when I wasn't in shape."

More than Your Bank Account

Tom's journey into passive income and eventually to BTR illustrates something people don't immediately see when they think of real estate.

It's not about the accounting.

It's not just about returns and appraised values and cash flow or amortization. Yes, those are real. Yes, those matter.

But they are not the *why*.

The *why* of real estate—and of this book—is that it *enables more important things*. Tom's real estate let him retire early, travel to spend time with every one of his kids, spend time with his wife, pursue his passion for flight, and feel and look younger at sixty than he did almost two decades earlier!

That is why passive income matters.

But there's more to the story. After all, BTR isn't the only way to generate passive income.

You could, after all, put all your money in the stock market. That's very passive. ETFs. Index funds. REITs. Bonds. Private equity. Private credit. There are all kinds of ways to invest.

Couldn't Tom just do *that* instead? And use the proceeds to fund a legendary family life?

The answer is yes. Of course, he could.

The argument for going the BTR route instead is twofold. The first reason to choose real estate goes all the way back to Chapter 1 and the five ways real estate makes money:

1. Appreciation. Real estate is an asset that rises in value over time.

2. Leverage. Unlike most other assets, like stocks, you can buy a lot of real estate for very little money.

3. Debt paydown. Over time, someone else (a tenant) pays for that real estate.

4. Tax benefits. There are many tax advantages specific to real estate, like depreciation, interest deduction on debt, and 1031 exchanges.

5. Cash flow. Real estate can put money in your pocket every month!

Tom got *every single one* of those benefits. That's tough to duplicate in the equity market. Most passive income investments hit two or perhaps three of those advantages. Certainly not all five.

But there's a second, less obvious reason, and it matters, too.

Your Investment Choices Matter

We used to build houses people could afford.

In the 1940s, the drive for home ownership was underway. The war had ended, the GI bill was in full swing, and the baby boom was beginning. Americans were hungry to own their own homes, and the builders of the nation were happy to oblige.

A "starter home"—let's call that a two- or three-bedroom house under 1400 square feet—was something that an average family could afford. Back then, almost 70% of homes fit that definition. A middle-class family could expect to save and buy a cheap and cheerful home that they could build equity in over time. It would shelter them, nurture their families, and give them a source of security in their golden years.

Things have changed. The number of new homes under 1,400 square feet has steadily declined for years. Paradoxically, the number of people in the giant new homes that replaced them is also shrinking. Effectively, we have half as many people living in houses twice as large!

There are many reasons for this. Rising land costs. Building restrictions. Increased construction costs. Car ownership. Changing wants. It's not hard to see why it happened.

What's important to note is that it's *changing again*. The boomers are downsizing. The Millennials and Gen Z-ers want a piece of the same dream.

But there's a challenge. At the time of this writing, the gap between the cost of owning and renting a home is wider than in more than fifteen years. Rising interest rates and increasing demand have increased home prices while rents have lagged.[8]

There are two stories here.

The first is that people still *want* homes. The dream of living in a house, having a yard, having an accessible neighborhood—that dream is still alive. But it's being challenged by economics.

The second story is that *investors like you can help*. There's an opportunity here to help people find homes that fit those dreams.

We *build* the homes people want. The homes are new, with high building standards and warranties. But most importantly, they are *median-sized*. They're homes that fill a huge need in the market. They're the homes where dreams can start.

When we bring BTR to a community, we *elevate* the community. We're increasing the supply of rental homes in places that need it most. Our tenants stay for the long-term, which increases both their security, and the stability of the community.

As an investor, you can use BTR not just to fuel your own legendary family life but to help others start the journey to their own. *That's* a benefit that's unique to BTR.

The Real in Real Estate

There is also a real estate story that lies beneath the surface of rents, mortgages, and cash flow.

Real estate can make you wealthy, deliver income, and help you create a truly astonishing life of abundance and joy for you and your family.

Or it can do the opposite.

Once we got our real estate in place, I could take adventures with my family. I could be there to give a kidney to my dad. We could give to charity, retire my parents. Real estate made that happen.

But before that, I was running. Always running. And it felt like running in place.

I can't imagine my life if we had stayed the course in those old houses. The flips and the bad tenants. The contractor scams and the difficult surprises. I would almost certainly have been able to build wealth had I continued on that route—and many people do—but it would have destroyed my family life.

Just because something is good at creating a living doesn't mean it's good at creating a *life*.

Once you know what you know, it's hard to go back. And I can't un-know that there's a better way to do real estate.

The Passive Income Playbook

I used to say that I rarely considered my net worth.

That wasn't quite true. The truth was that I was often *afraid* to look at my net worth. During the subprime mortgage crisis, it plummeted from about $4 million to *negative $3 million*. That period was so hard that it was easier to stop thinking about it altogether. I was just focused on surviving.

I imagine my dad had those moments, too. My parents never made more than $70,000 a year combined. They still had a home, and they raised a family. Life was fine. But money was a concern, and they never reached the level that my dad dreamed of.

Build-to-rent didn't exist when my dad was in his prime. He never had the opportunity I did. Fortunately, he benefitted from it through me. It took a generation longer than my dad had hoped, but eventually, we found our legendary family life.

So where have we arrived? In a nutshell:

•Real estate is a powerful wealth-creation tool. But it's also changing. The old Real Estate 1.0 model of old houses and flips simply doesn't generate *quality* passive income (low effort and predictable) the way it used to.

•Build-to-rent can solve the 1.0 problems and open the door to true passive income.

•That income, in turn, can be used to do the most important job in your life: strengthen your relationships.

It's a compelling argument. Here's the simple roadmap we recommend you use to put it to work:

1.Start by investing in a build-to-rent property with a trusted, established company. Your goal is to get to 3-5 properties.

2.Ensure that each deal meets the five success principles for passive income and avoids the five BTR traps.

3.Every 3-5 years, roll the equity in those properties into new deals.

4.Refinance over time, and let the rental income pay for your lifestyle—tax-free.

5.Use the four rhythms of legendary families to create lasting bonds with the people you love most.

And then? Repeat, and live out your legendary life.

The Passive Income Blueprint

1. Start by investing in a build-to-rent property with a trusted, established company. Your goal is to get to 3-5 properties.

2. Ensure that each deal meets the five success principles for passive income and avoids the 5 BTR traps.

3. Every 3-5 years, roll the equity in those properties into new deals.

4. Refinance over time, and let the rental income pay for your lifestyle—tax-free.

5. Use the four rhythms of legendary families to create lasting bonds with the people you love most.

CHAPTER ELEVEN

Legendary

Putting the Real in Real Estate

Remember Adam Hamilton? In Chapter 4, we met Adam as he discovered that his home area of Salt Lake City was becoming an increasingly challenging investment location.

Adam would eventually find his way to BTR in Florida. The locations he chose met all five success indicators for passive income. And it truly was *passive*—the difference was obvious in how little time Adam spent on his BTR investments versus the older properties he still owned.

That, however, is not the whole story.

On the surface, this is a real estate book. But it's really a book about your most important relationships. It's about reaching a place in your life, looking at your family, and knowing *you did the best with the time you have.*

In essence, this book is about living a life that offers you the great gift of *no regrets*. We just disguised it as a real estate book.

Which brings us back to Adam.

Adam found investment returns in BTR in another state. And he found fewer hassles, more predictability, and more freedom.

But it's what he *did* with those things that matters most.

The True Power of Real Estate

"When we started this journey," Adam recalled, "I had a pretty intense job. I worked an unreasonable amount for years. My oldest has memories of that.

"The passive income allowed me to walk away from a pretty high-paying job. It's allowed me to live next to family. I coach all three of my boys in every sport they want to do. I'm here when they leave for school. I'm here when they come home."

Thanks to passive income, Adam and his wife could homeschool during the pandemic. They took a six-week RV tour to visit Civil War historical sites. "The kids bring it up all the time," Adam said. "There's no way I would've been able to do that without that residual income."

Here, Adam paused in recounting the impact of BTR on his life.

"Had we not gone down the path of buying rental properties, specifically build-to-rent, which is probably the bulk of our portfolio," he paused again, "then we probably wouldn't have had our fourth child."

It's hard to overstate this. We know the Hamiltons. We know their kids. And right now, there is a beautiful small human who *exists because of their real estate choices.*

This *matters*. Real estate matters. Passive income matters. It brings people together. It changes lives.

And in Adam's case, it made new life possible.

"My dad was a boilermaker," he said, "and I was taught you go out, you get a job, and you just do everything they tell you. You hope you get a pay raise and hope that by the time you're my age, you can have half a million dollars stashed away so that you can make it until you die."

"I remember thinking, *really, is that the goal?*"

No. It isn't.

But we know what is.

The Goal

When we began this book journey, we started with a question: *who are our favorite, most successful BTR investors?*

We wanted to know what they had in common. After all—if we knew what brought them to us, and why they were thriving, it would help us reach more people like them.

We came up with a dozen names. They were all people who, after investing in their first BTR property, came right back to do the process again. They were happy and prosperous.

That made them great clients. But when we looked at the list, we realized something else: *11 out of 12 were involved in our family programs.*

These were people who came to our retreats. They used *The Family Board Meeting*. They had date nights.

They were, we realized, *people who shared our values.*

That insight has powered the writing of this book at a deep level.

I love Build-To-Rent. I love what it offers. As an investing approach, it's brought us an incredible amount of joy and freedom.

But we are a values-driven family, and we are a values-driven team. *That's* what matters most.

We wouldn't have it any other way.

Adam's story, and the ones like it, are *why we do this.* I will never, ever tire of messages like this one:

Thanks to you, I'm on a boat with my teenagers this week, having a remarkable family vacation.

We receive many. Each one is a gift. The investors, professionals, and entrepreneurs who write to us are discovering a new value to money. They are realizing that money is a tool, and the goal isn't simply *more.* The goal is to connect and strengthen what matters most in life.

They are also discovering one other thing that we'd be remiss not to mention: They're learning that there is no perfect family.

You may be nodding at that right now, thinking, *yes, there is no perfect family.*

But hear me: *There is no perfect family.*

If you're like me or the millions of others who have worked hard to find professional success and financial abundance, you've spent a lifetime trying to get things *as right as possible.* Which is a nice way of saying *trying to be perfect.*

Let that go.

Legendary family life isn't about perfection. It's about *bridging* our imperfections. It's about making the most of the precious time we have with the most important people in our world.

Don't put the pressure of perfection on yourself or your family. When you take that pressure away, something miraculous happens: *you begin to love being together.* And in a way, that's all that matters. That's the goal.

I've met and worked with thousands of families.

None of them are perfect. All of them are beautiful.

And they can all be legendary.

They just need a little time. *Your* time.

Are you willing to give it?

Your legendary family life awaits. We hope, with all our hearts, that you choose it.

- Jim & Jamie

Epilogue

Becoming Legendary

It's one of *those* tropical nights. The kind where the air is the same temperature as your skin, and you hardly know where your body ends and the world begins.

I park the car and walk through a grove of trees. There's just enough breeze to carry the smell of salt air. Through the palm leaves, a warm glow spread across the sky.

Red skies at night, sailor's delight.

It's an ancient mariner's expression, but it comes to life before me as I emerge from the trees to see the sunset blaze across the ocean.

To my right, a string of lights slopes lazily from one palm tree to another. In the distance, I can hear waves. It's a sound I love.

Beyond that is a sound I love even more: *laughter.*

I follow the string of lights, and the laughter grows. I hear murmurs of conversation. Then I emerge into a clearing.

In the center of the clearing, surrounded by palms, is a beautifully lit table with food and drink. Behind it is the beach and the deep red ocean, holding the last of the sunset.

Red skies at night.

Sitting at the table is my family. My brilliant and beautiful wife, Jamie. Our five kids, each unique and wondrous, each never failing to surprise me.

Sailor's delight.

Along with them are members of our team, some of our children's best friends, and local friends from Costa Rica, too. It's a beautiful blend of all the parts of our life, everyone gathered around one table, breaking bread. All laughing, smiling, nodding.

As I walk toward the table to join them, I am acutely aware of how remarkable this is. How extraordinary.

But there's a paradox here. Because I truly don't believe we are extraordinary. We're happy, yes. We've been fortunate, of course. But we've also done one thing, over and over: lived life according to a set of values that we believe in. We never chose to sacrifice family for finances. We never chose valuation over values. We refused to take revenue over relationships.

That's something everyone can aspire to.

Our legendary family life is, in this moment, what we dreamed it could be. As I reach the table and my waiting family, I think back to my father's unfulfilled promise, and it hits me. *I am living that promise.*

Just this morning, I walked a beautiful sand beach with Jamie—just like the couple on the card on my mother's dresser.

We had the same dream, my father and I. I was blessed to be able to take the torch and carry it.

The legendary family life my father dreamed of is here. Right now.

I could not be more grateful. Thank you for reading and joining us on this beautiful journey called life.

Before you go

One last thing.

We've been fortunate to bring build-to-rent to some of the top real estate experts, podcasts, and investor groups in the world. You probably recognize some of them:

GoBundance
EO (Entrepreneurs Org)
YPO
WCI – WhiteCoat
Jason Hartman/Empowered Investor
Get Rich Education
Real Estate Radio Guys
Real Wealth Network
Norada Real Estate
Yee Real Estate Network
Rock Star Inner Circle
Real Estate Rockstars
DLP
Family Offices
The West Experience(Aaron West)
MMT – Mastermind Talks

Freedom Founders

Bigger Pockets

Passive Income MD

Jake and Gino

The Redux Group

Rent to Retirement

Build2Rent

These groups and their content are a great way to learn. If you want to dive deeper into build-to-rent investing, you can book a free discovery call with us. We'll answer all your questions.

Just scan the code below!

—*Jim & Jamie*

Appendix A: The BTR Investor Process

*N*ote: *We're going to walk you through the BTR experience from the perspective of an investor. If you have questions, reach out anytime at 1-904-831-8019.*

Like many of our investors, Dave had some real estate experience. He'd done some fixer-uppers but found them time-consuming. As a dentist, he didn't want to spend his weekends working on his rental properties—he wanted real estate as a passive income investment, not a job.

That's where we came in!

- J & J

Step 1. Connection

Dave found us through my guest appearance on the Bigger-Pockets podcast. As is often the case when investors first hear about it, build-to-rent just seemed different to Dave. He'd had some challenges with his two previous properties, and BTR seemed like a solution.

That led him to one of our special reports, where he confirmed his first impressions and set up a discovery call with one of our head property consultants, Jennifer.

Step 2. Discovery Call

The first thing Dave wanted to know, naturally, was whether BTR was really going to be different than his fixer-uppers.

Jennifer has been with us for more than a dozen years. She knows her stuff. But she's also had her own experience with rehabs. She knows personally how new construction differs and answered all of Dave's questions about new builds and how passive the investment really is.

Step 3. Due Diligence

Convinced that BTR wasn't going to be a second job, Dave asked to see some numbers. Jennifer sent over what we call pro formas—documents that we use to show financial projections to investors so they can make good decisions. Dave reviewed them with his wife, Barbara. Barbara had seen the pressure he was under at work, and, like Dave, she was concerned this would create a second (or third!) job.

This is one of the biggest concerns with our clients, but it's also the problem that BTR is best able to solve. Jennifer sent over a few supporting videos comparing the time investment in BTR versus older properties.

Dave and Barbara were now confident that BTR was a viable path to true passive income. They arranged a video call with Jennifer to look at more detailed performance numbers for a sample duplex, including five-year projections with cash flow.

Step 4. Financing Part 1

One thing Barbara noted was that the mortgage interest rate we listed seemed to be a lot lower than what they were being quoted by their bank.

Jennifer explained we offer in-house financing where we pre-buy mortgages at much lower rates than those available to the public. The lender gets our stability and volume of business in exchange for low rates. We get to pass that on to investors to improve cash flow right from the start.

Step 5. Model & Location Choice

By the following week, Dave and Barbara were ready to move ahead. From our assortment of singles, duplexes, and quad models, they chose a duplex in Ocala for its inland location and excellent numbers. It was already under construction and close to completion.

From there, they were pleasantly surprised by how clear the next steps were. Unlike many real estate deals, our BTR process has been honed by thousands of builds and transactions, with a staff that walks the investor through every step and does all the heavy lifting.

Step 6. Financing Part 2

Once they chose their property, two things happened. First, they called to be pre-qualified with the preferred lender who offers our discounted rates. That took a whole ten minutes! Jennifer sent out a standard real estate agreement. They signed it digitally from their home and wired their 10% deposit the next day. Closing was only about 60 days off.

Step 7. Closing

Next, Dave and Barbara learned about our dedicated property management team and process. They spoke with a leasing specialist who explained exactly how the team would screen and find the best possible tenant. Meanwhile, Jennifer lined up the home inspection. The inspector noted one small item, which the builder immediately fixed.

Jennifer also arranged for an appraiser to visit the site. The appraisal actually came in a little bit over the sales price that we had agreed on!

Jennifer stayed in direct contact with Dave and Barbara right up to the closing and answered a few last questions, including every "what if" scenario that came to mind.

As the big day approached, Dave and Barbara received the closing statement estimate, which Jennifer reviewed with them. At closing, they sent over the final wire. We sent them our congratulations and a gift package.

And we also sent more good news: we'd already found a great tenant!

Step 8. The Passive Income Blueprint

Dave and Barbara's new Ocala income property was rented within two and a half weeks of the closing.

As a couple, they now spend 10-15 minutes a month reviewing their statement. If they have questions, they call their assigned portfolio manager, who knows them, the home, and the tenant.

Now, Dave and Barbara are looking for their second BTR property. They plan to follow the Passive Income Blueprint, rolling the equity in their properties into new deals every three to five years. They'll refinance over time and let the rental income pay for their lifestyle, tax-free. Then, they'll use that freedom to build their own legendary family life.

Appendix B: International Investors

*M*ore and more investors are not only crossing state lines to invest but international borders, too. Most of them are doing it for these reasons:

Affordability. The U.S. still has exceptional investment opportunities where investors can find both cash flow and appreciation.

Legislation. Landlord-friendly states make it easier to both collect and increase rents.

Availability. BTR is still relatively new in most of the world, especially outside of the U.K. and U.S.

U.S. dollar exposure. Having part of their portfolio connected to the world's reserve currency is a huge bonus for our international investors.

Every country has different rules, but there are some common steps when choosing to invest in the United States. What follows are the broad strokes for most international investors.

Every country is different—simply reach out if you have questions, and we'll connect you with the right professional.

-J & J

Step 1: Connect

Our team works with U.S. lenders who specialize in financing for international investors and have the best rates we've seen for foreign buyers. As of this writing, you do not need U.S. income or credit history to qualify.

Step 2: Professional Support

You'll need to have tax status in the U.S. to open a bank account and obtain financing here. For that, you'll want to use a U.S. accountant with experience. This process will get you the tax ID (ITIN #) you'll need to open a U.S. bank account in the next step.

You may still be required to file taxes in your home country. Your domestic accountant will interact with your U.S. accountant to ensure the job is completed correctly (and that you're not paying taxes twice!).

Step 3: Open a U.S. Bank Account

With the tax ID created in Step 2, you can open a U.S. account to manage the transaction and ongoing income.

Step 4: Choose your Property

Work with Southern Impression Homes to choose what location you'd like your investment property in and which property style!

Step 5: Sign and fund.

Sign an agreement to purchase and fund your U.S. bank account. Typically, you'll need closing costs, the down payment, and 12 months of reserves in the bank account 30 days prior to closing.

Step 6: Inspect and Appraise

Complete inspection and appraisal process—this clears the way for final financing and the close.

Step 7: Close

Onboard with Property Management, complete the closing, and take possession of your income property!

Endnotes

1. Rambaud, J. (2022, May 12). *Evolution of Rental Housing – The Rise of Build-For-Rent*. Halstatt Real Estate Partners. https://halstattrealestate.com/evolution-of-rental-housing-the-rise-of-build-for-rent/

2. Badger, E. (2022, September 25). Whatever Happened to the Starter Home. The New York Times. Retrieved from https://www.nytimes.com/2022/09/25/upshot/starter-home-prices.html

3. *Dr. David Phelps' Passion is Financial Planning for Dentists | Freedom Founders*. (2017, October 24). Freedom Founders | Dentists Building Wealth & Freedom Outside Wall Street. https://www.freedomfounders.com/our-story-retirement-for-dentists-orthodontists-old/david-phelps-story-financial-planning-for-dentists/

4. Peterson-Withorn, C. (2021, May 9). For Richer And Richest: Inside The Billion-Dollar Marriages, Open Relationships And Bitter Divorces Of The Forbes 400. Forbes Magazine. Retrieved from https://www.forbes.com/sites/chasewithorn/2021/05/09/bill-gates-divorce-inside-the-billion-dollar-marriages-most-expensive-divorces-bezos-divorce-harold-hamm-check/

5. Tyng, C. M., Amin, H. U., Saad, M. N. M., & Malik, A. S. (2017). The Influences of Emotion on Learning and Memory. Frontiers in psychology, 8, 1454. https://doi.org/10.3389/fpsyg.2017.01454

6. House, J. S., Landis, K. R., & Umberson, D. (1988). Social Relationships and Health. Science, 241(4865), 540-545. https://doi.org/10.1126/science.241.4865.540

7. Abadi, M., Snodgrass, E., Frias, L., Balevic, K., Getahun, H., & Vlamis, K. (2023, August 9). *20 lottery winners who lost it all — as someone in Florida just won the $1.58 billion Mega Millions jackpot*. Business Insider. https://www.businessinsider.com/lottery-winners-lost-everything-2017-8

8. *Putting Rent Increases into Perspective.* National Multifamily Housing Council. https://www.nmhc.org/research-insight/research-notes/2023/putting-rent-increases-into-perspective/

About the Authors

Jim Sheils has carved a niche in real estate with his profound expertise and strategic insights. As a pivotal partner at SI Homes, he has overseen significant property ventures, handling over $300 million in deals. His 23-year journey in real estate has been marked by a keen focus on generating passive income, facilitating both business growth and personal life enrichment through Build-To-Rent real estate.

Alongside real estate endeavors, Jim & Jamie founded 18 Summers, an initiative that echoes their commitment to helping families blend entrepreneurial zeal with deep family connections. Their collaborative effort in authoring *The Family Board Meeting*, a *Wall Street Journal* #1 best-seller, further exemplifies their dedication to mentoring families in achieving an integrative balance between professional pursuits and family life.

Together, Jim and Jamie Sheils are redefining the landscape of real estate success, paralleled by their passionate advocacy for nurturing strong, connected families.

CONNECT WITH
JIM & JAMIE

FOLLOW US ON YOUR FAVORITE SOCIAL MEDIA PLATFORMS

JJPLAYBOOK.COM

JIM SHEILS SPEAKS

LET JIM SHOW YOU HOW TO CREATE PASSIVE INCOME SO YOU CAN ENJOY A LEGENDARY FAMILY LIFE

JJPLAYBOOK.COM

Made in United States
Orlando, FL
02 February 2024

43203460R00098